EMANUEL SWEDENBORG

SPIRITUAL LEADERS AND THINKERS

JOHN CALVIN

DALAI LAMA (TENZIN GYATSO)

MARY BAKER EDDY

JONATHAN EDWARDS

DESIDERIUS ERASMUS

MOHANDAS GANDHI

AYATOLLAH RUHOLLAH KHOMEINI

MARTIN LUTHER

AIMEE SEMPLE McPHERSON

THOMAS MERTON

SRI SATYA SAI BABA

ELISABETH SCHÜSSLER FIORENZA

EMANUEL SWEDENBORG

SPIRITUAL
LEADERS AND
THINKERS

EMANUEL SWEDENBORG

Samuel Willard Crompton

Introductory Essay by
Martin E. Marty, Professor Emeritus
University of Chicago Divinity School

CHELSEA HOUSE
PUBLISHERS
A Haights Cross Communications Company

Philadelphia

COVER: Oil painting of Emanuel Swedenborg by Per Krafft the Elder (1724–1793).

CHELSEA HOUSE PUBLISHERS

VP, NEW PRODUCT DEVELOPMENT   Sally Cheney
DIRECTOR OF PRODUCTION   Kim Shinners
CREATIVE MANAGER   Takeshi Takahashi
MANUFACTURING MANAGER   Diann Grasse

Staff for EMANUEL SWEDENBORG

EXECUTIVE EDITOR   Lee Marcott
EDITOR   Kate Sullivan
PRODUCTION EDITOR   Noelle Nardone
PHOTO EDITOR   Sarah Bloom
SERIES AND COVER DESIGNER   Keith Trego
LAYOUT   21st Century Publishing and Communications, Inc.

First Printing

9 8 7 6 5 4 3 2 1

Library of Congress Cataloging-in-Publication Data

Crompton, Samuel Willard.
   Emanuel Swedenborg/by Samuel Willard Crompton.
      p. cm.—(Spiritual leaders and thinkers)
   ISBN 0-7910-8102-8
   1. Swedenborg, Emanuel, 1688-1772. I. Title. II. Series.
BX8748.C76 2004
289'.4'092—dc22

                                                            2004008475

CONTENTS

Foreword

W hy become acquainted with notable people when making efforts to understand the religions of the world?

Most of the faith communities number hundreds of millions of people. What can attention paid to one tell about more, if not most, to say nothing of *all*, their adherents? Here is why:

The people in this series are exemplars. If you permit me to take a little detour through medieval dictionaries, their role will become clear.

In medieval lexicons, the word *exemplum* regularly showed up with a peculiar definition. No one needs to know Latin to see that it relates to "example" and "exemplary." But back then, *exemplum* could mean something very special.

That "ex-" at the beginning of such words signals "taking out" or "cutting out" something or other. Think of to "excise" something, which is to snip it out. So, in the more interesting dictionaries, an *exemplum* was referred to as "a clearing in the woods," something cut out of the forests.

These religious figures are *exempla*, figurative clearings in the woods of life. These clearings and these people perform three functions:

First, they define. You can be lost in the darkness, walking under the leafy canopy, above the undergrowth, plotless in the pathless forest. Then you come to a clearing. It defines with a sharp line: there, the woods end; here, the open space begins.

Great religious figures are often stumblers in the dark woods.

We see them emerging in the bright light of the clearing, blinking, admitting that they had often been lost in the mysteries of existence, tangled up with the questions that plague us all, wandering without definition. Then they discover the clearing, and, having done so, they point our way to it. We then learn more of who we are and where we are. Then we can set our own direction.

Second, the *exemplum*, the clearing in the woods of life, makes possible a brighter vision. Great religious pioneers in every case experience illumination and then they reflect their light into the hearts and minds of others. In Buddhism, a key word is *enlightenment*. In the Bible, "the people who walked in darkness have seen a great light." They see it because their prophets or savior brought them to the sun in the clearing.

Finally, when you picture a clearing in the woods, an *exemplum*, you are likely to see it as a place of cultivation. Whether in the Black Forest of Germany, on the American frontier, or in the rain forests of Brazil, the clearing is the place where, with light and civilization, residents can cultivate, can produce culture. As an American moviegoer, my mind's eye remembers cinematic scenes of frontier days and places that pioneers hacked out of the woods. There, they removed stones, planted, built a cabin, made love and produced families, smoked their meat, hung out laundered clothes, and read books. All that can happen in clearings.

In the case of these religious figures, planting and cultivating and harvesting are tasks in which they set an example and then inspire or ask us to follow. Most of us would not have the faintest idea how to find or be found by God, to nurture the Holy Spirit, to create a philosophy of life without guidance. It is not likely that most of us would be satisfied with our search if we only consulted books of dogma or philosophy, though such may come to have their place in the clearing.

Philosopher Søren Kierkegaard properly pointed out that you cannot learn to swim by being suspended from the ceiling on a belt and reading a "How To" book on swimming. You learn because a parent or an instructor plunges you into water, supports you when necessary, teaches you breathing and motion, and then releases you to swim on your own.

Kierkegaard was not criticizing the use of books. I certainly have nothing against books. If I did, I would not be commending this series to you, as I am doing here. For guidance and courage in the spiritual quest, or—and this is by no means unimportant!—in intellectual pursuits, involving efforts to understand the paths others have taken, there seems to be no better way than to follow a fellow mortal, but a man or woman of genius, depth, and daring. We "see" them through books like these.

Exemplars come in very different styles and forms. They bring differing kinds of illumination, and then suggest or describe diverse patterns of action to those who join them. In the case of the present series, it is possible for someone to repudiate or disagree with *all* the religious leaders in this series. It is possible also to be nonreligious and antireligious and therefore to disregard the truth claims of all of them. It is more difficult, however, to ignore them. Atheists, agnostics, adherents, believers, and fanatics alike live in cultures that are different for the presence of these people. "Leaders and thinkers" they may be, but most of us do best to appraise their thought in the context of the lives they lead or have led.

If it is possible to reject them all, it is impossible to affirm everything that all of them were about. They disagree with each other, often in basic ways. Sometimes they develop their positions and ways of thinking by separating themselves from all the others. If they met each other, they would likely judge each other cruelly. Yet the lives of each and all of them make a contribution to the intellectual and spiritual quests of those who go in ways other than theirs. There are tens of thousands of religions in the world, and millions of faith communities. Every one of them has been shaped by founders and interpreters, agents of change and prophets of doom or promise. It may seem arbitrary to walk down a bookshelf and let a finger fall on one or another, almost accidentally. This series may certainly look arbitrary in this way. Why precisely the choice of these exemplars?

In some cases, it is clear that the publishers have chosen someone who has a constituency. Many of the world's 54 million Lutherans may be curious about where they got their name, who the man Martin Luther was. Others are members of a community but choose isolation: The hermit monk Thomas Merton is typical. Still others are exiled and achieve their work far from the clearing in which they grew up; here the Dalai Lama is representative. Quite a number of the selected leaders had been made unwelcome, or felt unwelcome in the clearings, in their own childhoods and youth. This reality has almost always been the case with women like Mary Baker Eddy or Aimee Semple McPherson. Some are extremely controversial: Ayatollah Ruhollah Khomeini stands out. Yet to read of this life and thought as one can in this series will be illuminating in much of the world of conflict today.

Reading of religious leaders can be a defensive act: Study the lives of certain ones among them and you can ward off spiritual— and sometimes even militant—assaults by people who follow them. Reading and learning can be a personally positive act: Most of these figures led lives that we can indeed call exemplary. Such lives can throw light on communities of people who are in no way tempted to follow them. I am not likely to be drawn to the hermit life, will not give up my allegiance to medical doctors, or be successfully nonviolent. Yet Thomas Merton reaches me and many non-Catholics in our communities; Mary Baker Eddy reminds others that there are more ways than one to approach healing; Mohandas Gandhi stings the conscience of people in cultures like ours where resorting to violence is too frequent, too easy.

Finally, reading these lives tells something about how history is made by imperfect beings. None of these subjects is a god, though some of them claimed that they had special access to the divine, or that they were like windows that provided for illumination to that which is eternal. Most of their stories began with inauspicious childhoods. Sometimes they were victimized, by parents or by leaders of religions from which they later broke.

Some of them were unpleasant and abrasive. They could be ungracious toward those who were near them and impatient with laggards. If their lives were symbolic clearings, places for light, many of them also knew clouds and shadows and the fall of night. How they met the challenges of life and led others to face them is central to the plot of all of them.

I have often used a rather unexciting concept to describe what I look for in books: *interestingness*. The authors of these books, one might say, had it easy, because the characters they treat are themselves so interesting. But the authors also had to be interesting and responsible. If, as they wrote, they would have dulled the personalities of their bright characters, that would have been a flaw as marring as if they had treated their subjects without combining fairness and criticism, affection and distance. To my eye, and I hope in yours, they take us to spiritual and intellectual clearings that are so needed in our dark times.

Martin E. Marty
The University of Chicago

1

Dreams and Visions

It were best to die before by way of hoary locks,
wrinkles and languid powers the transit is
made to cold and weary death.

—Emanuel Swedenborg in his graduation speech

E manuel Swedenborg was in Holland in the spring of 1744. Holland was the land of tulips, canals, and slow, winding country lanes. Swedenborg loved Holland and praised the country in his writings:

> I here considered why it was that it has pleased our Lord to bless such an uncouth and avaricious people with such a splendid economy; why He has preserved them for such a long time from all misfortunes; and has caused them to surpass all other nations in commerce and enterprise. . . . The principal cause seems to me to have been that it is a republic, wherein the Lord delights more than in monarchical coun-tries; as also appears from Rome. The result is that no one deems himself obliged and in duty bound to accord honor and veneration to any human being.[1]

Swedenborg's native Sweden was different from Holland both in geography and the ways of the people who lived there. Sweden was the land of sharp fjords, breathtaking views, and rugged mountain passes. Such a sharp and steep landscape made for a sturdy independence among the people, but they had not been able to join or to capitalize on the republican form of govern-ment or the prosperity enjoyed by Holland.

Swedenborg had always been an independent thinker in terms of science, his chosen vocation. But now, in the spring of 1744, he was about to have a spontaneous initiation into mystical depths. Like the Dutch people whom he so much respected, Swedenborg would need all his courage and independence of mind. He had been raised as a pious Lutheran, and his new adventure was about to contradict much of what he had been taught about religion and faith.

Clues about this initiation come from Swedenborg's descrip-tion of a dream he had on March 25, 1744:

> I asked for a cure against my illness, and I was offered a heap of rags to buy. I took half of them and selected from the other

half, but finally I gave back all the rags. He said that he would himself buy me something that would lead to a cure. The rags were my corporeal thoughts by which I wished to cure myself, but they were good for nothing.[2]

Swedenborg was usually in the best of health, and it is unknown what illness he had. The mystery continued to unfold, with a spectacular dream on Sunday, April 4, which was Easter. Twenty-four hours later came another set of dreams. In his dream diary, Swedenborg wrote the abbreviation "N.B." three times next to this entry. This two-letter combination is the abbreviated form of the Latin expression *Nota Bene*, which means "Note Well" in English. Clearly, Swedenborg considered this set of dreams to be the most significant:

> In the evening I came into another sort of temptation, namely, between eight and nine in the evening, while I read about God's miracles performed through Moses. I observed that something of my own understanding interfered and made it impossible for me really to believe this as I should; I both believed and not believed at the same time. I thought this is the reason that the angels and God showed themselves to shepherds and not to philosophers, who let their understanding enter into these matters. . . . At ten o'clock I went to bed and felt a little better. After half an hour, I heard some din under my head, and then I thought that the tempter left. Immediately a shiver came over me, starting from the head and spreading throughout the body, with some rumbling, coming in waves, and I realized that something holy had befallen me.[3]

These entries reveal a profound sense of loneliness. Swedenborg was on his own; no one could help him against these spirits or tempters that tormented him:

> Whereupon I went to sleep, and about twelve o'clock, or perhaps it was one or two in the morning, such a strong

shivering seized me, from my head to my feet, as a thunder produced by several clouds colliding, shaking me beyond description and prostrating me. And when I was prostrated in this way, I was clearly awake and saw how I was overthrown.[4]

He lay on the floor, trying to gain control over his thoughts:

I wondered what this was supposed to mean, and I spoke as if awake but found that the words were put into my mouth. I said, "Oh, thou almighty Jesus Christ, who of thy great mercy designest to come to so great a sinner, make me worthy of this grace!" and I clasped my hands and prayed. Then a hand emerged, which pressed my hands firmly. In a little while I continued in prayer, saying, "Thou hast promised to receive in grace all sinners; thou canst not otherwise than keep thy words!" In the same moment I was sitting in his bosom and beheld him face to face, a countenance of a holy mien. All was such that I cannot describe. He was smiling at me, and I was convinced that he looked like this when he was alive. He spoke to me and asked if I have a health certificate; and to this I replied, "Lord, thou knowest better than I." He said, "Well then, do!"—that is, as I inwardly grasped this, "Do love me," or "Do as promised." God give me grace thereto! I found it beyond my powers and work up, shuddering.[5]

Countless studies of Swedenborg and his dreams have commented on the words "a health certificate." Was this in some way a dream return to an incident in Swedenborg's youth when he had jumped quarantine in London, never receiving a clean bill of health? Or was it a much greater statement, one from God, which required him to know the state of his health: mental, psychological, and physical?

Then there was another powerful phrase: "I observed that something of my own understanding interfered and made it impossible for me really to believe this as I should." Did this refer to Swedenborg's upbringing as the son of a Lutheran bishop?

Or did it mean that his years as a successful man of science made it hard for him to delve into spiritual mysteries?

And finally there were those direct words from God: "Well then, do!"

Could there be any stronger statement?

This was a dramatic moment. Swedenborg had met the holiest of holies. Whether he continued with his scientific work or not, he had been launched onto the path of mysticism.

Young Swedenborg and Old Sweden

*[W]hen they saw me coming, as they afterwards
told me, they quivered more than they ever
did before the enemy. . . .*

—The Reverend Jesper Swedenborg

Every person, with rare exceptions, is both a product of his or her times and also a rebel against them. The competing desires to conform to what is and to rebel against it are familiar to most people. These desires played out in the early life of Emanuel Swedenborg.

FATHER AND SON

Emanuel Svedberg was born in Stockholm, Sweden, on January 29, 1688. He was the third child of Jesper Svedberg and Sarah Behm. After Emanuel's birth, the couple had six more children. They were, in order of their birth, Albert, Anna, Emanuel, Hedvig, Daniel, Eliezer, Catharina, Jesper, and Margaretha.[6] Albert died in 1696, making Emanuel the oldest son in the family.

Svedberg was the family's original name. The ending, "berg," means hill. All the family members carried this surname until 1719, when they were ennobled by the Swedish Crown. This honor resulted in the family name changing to Swedenborg, whose ending, "borg," means castle.

Jesper Svedberg, the family patriarch, retained his original surname, for as a leader in the Lutheran Church, he could not be ennobled. A powerful and influential man, he came from a family of copper miners who had prospered during the seventeenth century. Jesper Svedberg was the first member of his family to enter the ministry when, in 1682, he was ordained in the Swedish Lutheran Church.

Soon after his ordination, the Reverend Svedberg married Sarah Behm. She, too, came from a family that was intimately involved with mining, the principal source of wealth in Sweden. Her father was an assessor for the Royal Bureau of Mines, and Sarah brought considerable wealth to her marriage. This was fortunate for Jesper Svedberg, who often outspent his income, especially when it came to his voluminous writings. He published many of these at his own expense and spent a great deal of money in the process.

Very little is known of Emanuel Swedenborg's early years. It is likely that he saw rather little of his father, who took a new position as chaplain to the king's regiment of Life Guards. Swedenborg grew up in a large and close family, however, and he was especially fond of his older sister, Anna. The pair likely spent many summer hours carousing in the luxurious Swedish sunlight and many winter days huddling together against the frigid cold and oppressive darkness.

Because he left behind a 1,000-page autobiography, we know more about the Reverend Jesper Svedberg during these years than we do about Emanuel or any other members of the family. Jesper Svedberg was a tall and imposing man, and he made the most of his new job as chaplain to the king's guards. Years later, he described what it was like for the guards to come before him and perform their catechism:

> To this they were quite unused, so that when they saw me coming, as they afterwards told me, they quivered more than they ever did before the enemy; but when I commenced telling them in a quiet way stories from the Bible, and strengthening them in Christian faith and life, they began to like me so well that they did not care to go away when their time was up and another detachment was coming in [there were 1,200 of the Life Guards], so that between the two I was nearly trampled down.[7]

Another story about the elder Svedberg concerns some special taxes that King Charles XI was about to levy on the Swedish people. When Svedberg preached his next sermon, it was obvious through the Bible passage he chose to discuss that Svedberg opposed the new taxies or levies:

> Ye hate the good and love the evil; ye pluck off their skin from them and their flesh from off their bones, and eat the flesh of my people; and when ye have flayed their skin from off them, ye break their bones also in pieces.[8]

An officer of the royal guards asked King Charles XI, "Shall the parson speak in this style?"[9]

The king replied: "Did the parson confirm his sermon by God's Word? . . . If the parson has God's Word, the King has nothing to say against it."[10]

On another occasion, King Charles XI told the Reverend Svedberg that he had made enemies through some other sermons. The reverend replied that it was a sorry man of God who did not do so for the powers of religion were always arrayed against those of the world.

It is easy to be impressed with Jesper Svedberg's courage, but one should take into account that the reverend was himself something of a man of the world. He loved attention, which he gained through his powerful sermons, and he loved to disturb people who seemed to be at peace in their lives. In his long autobiography, Svedberg described how the people of Uppsala welcomed him when he was made rector of the university there in 1695:

> I experienced this grace from God, that there was such unity
> and trust among the teachers that there was never any
> dissension. . . . When both my buildings were burned down,
> in the great conflagration after Ascension-day, the students
> manifested themselves towards me so much kindness, carry-
> ing out and saving everything except the fixtures, that, thank
> God! I suffered little harm; and such pure affection they
> constantly exhibited towards me during the whole of my
> stay amongst them.[11]

Clearly, Svedberg knew how to congratulate himself. Knowing students and universities as we do, however, it seems very unlikely that the 10 years he served as the university's rector would have passed without any student disturbances.

Sarah Behm died in 1696. She was only 30 and had given birth to nine children. The Reverend Svedberg praised his deceased wife to the heavens, but soon took a second one. Sara Bergia was yet another daughter of a wealthy mine owner. Jesper Svedberg obtained a good deal of money through the marriage, but he was most interested in having a good second mother for his children. Sara Bergia, who had been unable to bear children in her previous marriage, was a good mother to her stepchildren. Emanuel appears to have been her favorite.[12]

The Svedberg family experienced loss when their mother died in 1696 and experienced a rebirth of sorts when their father remarried in 1697. Almost the same thing happened for the nation as a whole, which lost one monarch in the spring of 1697 and found a new one that Christmas.

THE WARRIOR KING

King Charles XI died of natural causes in March 1697. He was only in middle age, but he was worn out from the cares and demands of the monarchy. Because the deceased king had been an excellent patron to the Reverend Svedberg, there was some concern in the Svedberg family, but no unpleasant changes occurred. Sweden as a whole welcomed the accession of King Charles XII, who was crowned on Christmas Day, 1697.[13]

Charles was only 15 when he took the throne. There was serious concern that such a young monarch might not be able to defend the realm, but this fear proved groundless. Descended from a line of warrior-kings, Charles soon proved himself worthy of his ancestors.

The turn of the eighteenth century brought a change in fortunes both for the Svedberg family and for Sweden in general. In 1700, King Charles XII went to war with Denmark, Poland, and Russia. Sweden had been the dominant power in the Baltic Sea for almost a century, and King Charles wanted to keep it that way.

UNIVERSITY OF UPPSALA

At about the same time, the Reverend Svedberg was elevated to the position of bishop in the Swedish Lutheran Church. This was the apex of success as far as he was concerned; there were only seven bishops in all of Sweden. King Charles XII granted Bishop Svedberg a diocese in the countryside, and most of the Svedberg family moved there around 1703. Emanuel did not, however. He remained in Uppsala where he lived with his older sister, Anna, and her new husband, Eric Benzelius.[14]

About 15 years older than Emanuel, Eric Benzelius soon became like a second father. Jesper Svedberg had always been most interested in public matters, and his family life had suffered correspondingly. Benzelius, who was the chief librarian at the University of Uppsala, was able to give more affection and direction to the young Emanuel than his natural father ever had.

By 1704, Emanuel Swedenborg was listed in the rolls of Uppsala University as a freshman. He appears to have made rather slow academic progress. One might wonder at this, considering that later generations have estimated his intelligence quotient (IQ) to be over 200. (A person with an IQ of 140 or higher is typically considered a genius.) Like many brilliant people, however, Emanuel Swedenborg was a slow developer. He may well have

EIGHTEENTH-CENTURY COLLEGES

Swedenborg attended the University of Uppsala, Sweden's premier institution of higher learning. At the time, there were only three colleges in the American colonies: Harvard, founded in 1636; William and Mary, founded in 1692; and Yale, founded in 1718.

Because Latin and Greek were the backbone of the college curriculum, scholars in Sweden, England, and America would probably have found that they had much in common. At Harvard College, a student could be fined for speaking English rather than Latin in the courtyard now known as Harvard Yard. The few hundred, and later few thousand, college students in America were more like English or even Swedish college students than their uneducated neighbors back home.

Latin and Greek were still studied throughout the eighteenth and nineteenth centuries. During the American Revolution of 1775 and the French Revolution of 1789, national languages, like English and French, became more important and reduced the emphasis on Latin and Greek. By about 1850, college students did their work in their respective national languages, and the international community of scholars who wrote in Latin virtually disappeared. Swedenborg and his fellow students did not foresee this development, however. They expected that educated people around the world would continue to use Latin as the language for educated conversation and exchange.

needed to get out of the presence of his impressive father just to begin his own progress.

Uppsala was one of only two universities in all of Sweden. The campus had about 1,000 students and a faculty of about 10 professors with numerous support staff. The Swedes were painfully conscious of the fact that they were behind the rest of Western Europe in terms of academic achievement; Sweden, after all, had not produced major intellectual figures like John Locke or Isaac Newton. About the only major international figure to have come to Uppsala had been the French philosopher René Descartes, about 50 years earlier.

Leaders of the university like Eric Benzelius were very ambitious for the school. They wanted its students to take their places among the great learned men of Europe at the time, and the best way to do so was to have them study the works of thinkers such as Descartes, Newton, and Locke.

Descartes had led the way. In 1619, he had published his masterwork, which contained the radical phrase, "I think, therefore I am." This bald statement of pure consciousness has been taken ever since as one of the basic creeds of intellectual life. Descartes's thinking, known as Cartesian thought, predominated at the University of Uppsala.

Isaac Newton had, in 1687, published his own masterwork—*The Principia* (or *Principles of Natural Philosophy*). Newton had expanded on the work of Galileo (1564–1642) in the investigation of the earth, moon, and planets. Newton had formulated the law of gravity and had also made postulates such as "for every action there is a counter-action." Newton portrayed a beautiful universe, one in which all things cooperated and responded to one another, but his critics claimed that he deadened the universe by making it too mechanical.

John Locke had published his great work in 1690. Locke's *An Essay Concerning Human Understanding* remains one of the most intriguing and yet baffling of all great philosophical works. Locke claimed that the human being came into the world as a *tabula rasa* ("blank slate") and that an individual was therefore the product of his or her experiences. This was a bold departure from Christian scripture, which taught that men and women came into the world already shaped by God. Locke was not antireligious—far from it. Like most of the philosophers of his day, he believed in God. Locke, however, wanted there to be room for science as well.

The opinions of Descartes had originally been considered so revolutionary that they had been banned from the Uppsala campus. In 1689, however, just one year after Emanuel Swedenborg's birth, the king had decreed that the new scientific thoughts could be taught as long as they did not directly contradict the Bible.

In spite of the king's tolerance for new thinking and scientific ideas, the new century brought hard times for the University of Uppsala. Historian Sten Lindroth explained:

> In May 1702, Uppsala was ravaged by a devastating fire, which in a short time reduced the greater part of the town to ashes. Many of the professors . . . lost all their possessions; the Cathedral was badly damaged, but fortunately the Gusavianum [the university's main building] was saved.[15]

Not a great deal is known about Emanuel Swedenborg's years at the university. It is very likely that he studied the works of Descartes and Locke, and we know that he developed a special reverence for Isaac Newton. For the most part, however, his studies revolved around the writings and thought of the classical world: those of ancient Greece and Rome. He learned Latin and Greek and performed better at Hebrew than most of his fellow students. Though he had a slight stammer, Swedenborg loved to present material at academic sessions and was occasionally chastised for being too forward.

Swedenborg loved learning for its own sake. Like many young men of his day, he was excited by the possibilities of the new science (there was no strict separation between science and philosophy at the time), which was peeking around the corner from the walls created by the Middle Ages, an era during which the Church so discouraged scientific progress, fearing that it challenged the sovereignty of God, that we now refer to this time as the "Dark Ages." When Swedenborg attended Uppsala, however, Europeans were starting to enter the light of what was later called the "Age of Reason."

GRADUATION SPEECH

The University of Uppsala held its graduation on the first day of June in 1709. Twenty-two-year-old Emanuel Swedenborg stepped up to deliver one of the graduation speeches, known at that time as a disputation.

Swedenborg had chosen the sayings of Seneca and Publilius Syrus, two ancient Roman philosophers, as the background for his speech (to learn more about these philosophers, simply enter their names and the keywords "roman philosophy" into any Internet search engine and browse the sites listed). Since European universities venerated the classical tradition of Greece and Rome, this was not an unusual choice. Swedenborg started with the philosophers' words on love: "Time not mind makes an end to love. . . . Love cannot be wrenched away, it can slip away. . . . Tears of love rise in the eyes, they fall in the breast."[16]

It is not known to what extent Swedenborg had yet experienced love. He was a handsome young man, but he had led a sheltered life, first as the favored son of a bishop and then as the protégé of his academic brother-in-law.

The next theme of Swedenborg's speech was friendship. He quoted Seneca: "Friendship is always helpful, love can be injurious. . . . To injure a friend even in jest in not permissible. . . . He who is a friend loves; he who loves is not always a friend."[17]

Again, we are uncertain to what extent Swedenborg was speaking from experience. We do not know whether he had yet formed deep friendships outside of his own family. Friendship, however, would remain one of the central themes of his life.

Emanuel Swedenborg then used the philosophers' ideas to introduce a discussion on greed: "Money only irritates the miser; it doesn't content him. . . . What ill do you wish a miser but a long life? . . . The benevolent discover chances to give."[18]

Swedenborg had little money at this time in his life, but he stood to inherit from the wealth of his mother and stepmother's family mines. Much to Emanuel's dismay, his father, despite being a minister, was deeply attached to money.

Swedenborg ended his speech with some thoughts on death: "While life is welcome is the best time for death. . . . It were best to die before by way of hoary locks, wrinkles and languid powers the transit is made to cold and weary death."[19]

What, though, did young Swedenborg really know about death? He knew about it only from books. By contrast, thousands of Swedes, many of them even younger than Swedenborg, were about to learn about death firsthand, in a far-off place called Poltava.

After the graduation ceremony, Swedenborg accepted the congratulations of faculty, family, and friends. His graduation marked his entrance into the community of scholars at Sweden's greatest seat of learning.

SWEDEN'S YOUNG MEN AT POLTAVA

In the same month that Swedenborg gave his graduation speech, thousands of young Swedes were fighting for their lives at a distant place in the Ukraine, called Poltava.

King Charles XII had invaded Russia in 1708. He and his men suffered through the terrible winter. Spring eventually came, and King Charles and his loyal Swedes besieged the Russian-held Poltava. The siege began in May, and while Emanuel Swedenborg delivered his academic disputation at Uppsala, King Charles and his men awaited the approach of Tsar Peter (known as Peter the Great) and the Russian army.

The battle began at about 5:00 A.M. on June 28, 1709. Even though he was outnumbered and even though the Russians were well dug in, King Charles decided to attack.[20] Attack, attack, attack had always been his watchwords, and they had served him well to this point. Under his leadership, Swedish soldiers had become feared for their bravery and skill under fire.

King Charles, who had been wounded a few weeks earlier, observed the assault from a litter on which he was brought to the battlefield. He was soon dismayed, as were his men, by the volume of cannon fire from the Russian lines. Tsar Peter had created an artillery park and his guns were wreaking havoc on the Swedes.

It was all over in about two hours. Thousands of other Swedes lay dead on the battlefield. Tsar Peter had won his showdown with the Swedish king. With his army in ruins, Charles escaped to Turkey, where he was forced to remain for almost five years.[21]

Meanwhile, young Emanuel Swedenborg had left home as well, headed for a tour of the scientific capitals of Western Europe. The trip would mark the beginning of a brilliant—and extremely diverse—career.

3

Adventures
Abroad

*You encourage me to go on with my studies; but I think
I ought rather to be discouraged, as I have such
"immoderate desire" for them, especially for
astronomy and mechanics.*

—Emanuel Swedenborg in a letter to his brother-in-law

In the summer of 1710, just one year after delivering his graduation speech, Emanuel Swedenborg left Sweden and headed for England, the home of Newton, Locke, and other great thinkers of the time. Years later, Swedenborg recalled his first international voyage:

> In 1710 I set out for Gottenburg, that I might be conveyed by a ship thence to London. . . . in London itself I was exposed to a more serious danger. While we were entering the harbor, some of our countrymen came to us in a boat and persuaded me to go with them into the city. Now, it was known in London that [the plague] was raging in Sweden; therefore all who arrived from Sweden were forbidden to leave their ships for six weeks or forty days; so I, having transgressed this law, was very near being hanged, and was only freed under the condition that if any one attempted the same things again, he should not escape the gallows.[22]

Swedenborg was not exaggerating the danger of the plague. Bubonic plague was less common in Europe than it had been one to two hundred years earlier, but Sweden was hit with an especially virulent epidemic in 1710. The city of Stockholm lost about 15,000 people out of 60,000. All in all, this was probably a very good time for Swedenborg to be abroad rather than in his homeland (to learn more about this epidemic, simply enter the keywords "bubonic plague Sweden 1700s" into any Internet search engine and browse the sites listed).

Swedenborg settled into quarters in a working-class section of London. He had only about 250 Swedish *thalers* (it is difficult to determine how much this old Swedish currency would equal in today's dollars) on which to live, a meager amount for the time. By employing the versatility and adaptability that would become his hallmark, he lived better than the sum would indicate. In part, this was because of his social connections. Bishop Jesper Svedberg was known not only in Sweden but also in the Swedish communities in other nations. Emanuel Swedenborg was therefore welcomed and assisted by the Swedish community in London. He was a young man on the first major adventure of his life, and what a place he had chosen to explore!

LONDON IN 1710

London was the center of a bustling international trade. The English and Scots (who were now called collectively the "British") had become the foremost merchant brokers of their day. The Thames River was crowded with ships that brought sugar from the Caribbean, tobacco from America, and tea from far-off India.

Swedenborg was never very interested in trade or making money, but he recognized that England's position as the center of world trade had contributed to making the nation a leader in international science as well. One hand fed the other, and Swedenborg was pleased to be at the center of the action. His first letter to his brother-in-law, Eric Benzelius, was written on October 13, 1710:

> Dearest Brother
>
> . . . This island . . . has also men of the greatest experience in this science, but these I have not yet consulted, because I am not sufficiently acquainted with their language. I study Newton [who wrote in Latin rather than in English] daily, and am very anxious to see and hear him. . . .
>
> Whatever is worthy of being seen in the town, I have already examined. The magnificent St. Paul's cathedral was finished a few days ago in all its parts. In examining the royal monuments in Westminster Abbey, I happened to see the tomb of Casaubon; when I was inspired with such a love for this literary hero, that I kissed his tomb, and dedicated to his names, under the marble, the following stanzas:
>
> *Why adornest thou the tomb with marble, with song, and with gold?*
>
> *When yet these will perish and thou wilt survive. But, methinks the marble and gold for their sakes praise thee.*
>
> *For the marble loves the kisses of the passers by.* [23]

Very few diary entries or letters could capture the young Swedenborg so aptly as this one. He was a young man in love with learning for the sake of learning. He admired the essayist Isaac Casaubon more than any of the kings, queens, or statesmen honored in Westminster Abbey.

Swedenborg became quite involved with his studies in London; he learned English rapidly and was soon able to read Locke, Newton, and others in their native language (by the end of his long life, Swedenborg would master 10 languages).

Swedenborg was especially drawn to Newton's ideas. In 1687, Newton had published his *Principia*, one of the landmark books in the history of the natural sciences. In the book, Newton laid out his vision of a universe that operated on mechanical principles, one in which every action had a reaction and where the forces of nature were continually balanced and rebalanced. It was this natural philosophy that excited Swedenborg.

Swedenborg was also excited by the ideas of John Locke. Twenty years earlier, in 1690, Locke had published his two masterworks: *Two Treatises of Government* and *Essay Concerning*

LONDON IN 1710–1715

Between 1710 and 1715, London was probably the most exciting city on Earth. Queen Anne was on the throne, England was winning the War of the Spanish Succession, and the merchant trade of London thrived. In the world of art, music, and science, London was becoming the preeminent city of Western culture.

The German musician George Handel arrived in London in 1711, just one year after Swedenborg. The English artist William Hogarth was about to perfect his series of lithographs of low-down life in London. Isaac Newton was still alive. London had become the center around which science and art in the Western world revolved.

Of course there was a "dirty" part or "underside" to the story. Hogarth's paintings show a city full of poor, ragged people drinking themselves to death with gin. This cheap liquor became the rage in London about the time that Swedenborg arrived there; he does not seem to have had any attraction toward strong spirits.

Rather, Swedenborg spent his time in London dedicated to improving his mind and taking advantage of all the opportunities the sophisticated city had to offer.

Human Understanding. The publication of these two books, along with Newton's *Principia*, is usually considered the beginning of the European Enlightenment.

Although Locke was dead by 1710 and Swedenborg never fulfilled his desire to meet Sir Isaac Newton, other scientists were quite willing to meet the young Swede. As they came to know him, he rose in their estimation. One of these was Sir Edmond Halley, who discovered the comet that now bears his name; the other was John Flamsteed, one of the leaders of the English Royal Society.

Swedenborg wrote again to his brother-in-law in April 1711, about nine months after his arrival in England:

> I visit daily the best mathematicians here in town. I have been with [John] Flamsteed, who is considered the best astronomer in England, and who is constantly taking observations which, together with the Paris observations, will give us some day a correct theory respecting the motion of the moon and of its appulse to the fixed stars. . . . You encourage me to go on with my studies; but I think I ought rather to be discouraged, as I have such an "immoderate desire" for them, especially for astronomy and mechanics. I also turn my lodgings to some use, and change them often. At first I was at a watchman's, afterwards at a cabinetmaker's, and now I am at a mathematical-instrument maker's. From them I steal their trades, which some day will be of use to me. I have recently computed for my own pleasure several useful tables for the latitude of Upsal, and all the solar and lunar eclipses, which will take place between 1712 and 1721.[24]

It is fairly obvious from this letter that Swedenborg was not a typical young man interested in wine, women, and song. Instead, he longed and hungered for knowledge.

Swedenborg and John Flamsteed, the astronomer mentioned in the young man's letter, made an odd scientific couple. Flamsteed, a rather crusty old man, had spent years upon years gazing at the stars, and there were many who said that his mind had gone. During the time that Swedenborg was in London, John Flamsteed was embroiled in a long controversy with Sir Isaac Newton and Edmond Halley, who insisted that he publish the results of his stargazing. Flamsteed protested long and loudly that he was not yet finished, but Newton and Halley eventually stole his research and published it themselves, a sad commentary about cooperation among scientists in the Age of Reason. Nonetheless, Flamsteed had a profound influence on young Swedenborg.

Flamsteed took Swedenborg on as an assistant. Swedenborg often worked the night shift at the Royal Observatory at Greenwich, cataloging stars and celestial movements. It was an exciting time in science, and Swedenborg could hardly have found a more distinguished employer than Flamsteed. It was while working at the Royal Observatory at Greenwich (where the prime meridian is located today) that Swedenborg put his brain to work on one of the most prickly scientific problems of the day: finding longitude.

THE LONGITUDE

By 1700, sailors could usually find their latitude while at sea, but determining their longitude remained a constant difficulty. Many ships went astray and were wrecked because those sailing in them did not know their longitudinal (east to west) position. The worst disaster of the age had occurred in 1707 when Admiral Sir Cloudesly Shovell went onto the rocks of the Scilly Isles off England's western coast. About 2,000 sailors drowned that day. Shovell survived to drift ashore, where he was promptly murdered by a thief. The disaster led the British parliament to offer the hefty reward of 20,000 pounds sterling to the person who figured out a way to determine a ship's longitude. Many methods were proposed; one of them involved ships at sea firing cannons that could be heard for hundreds of miles. By firing only on the hour and half-hour, they believed they could spread the correct time around the globe.[25]

With Flamsteed's encouragement, Swedenborg developed the novel idea of trying to find longitude by calculations based on the moon. Around this time, he wrote home to his brother-in-law. Among other things, the letter suggests that Bishop Svedberg kept his son on a tight financial leash:

> I have not met with great encouragement here in England, among this civil and proud people, I have laid it aside for some other place. When I tell them I have some project about longitude, they treat it as an impossibility; and so I do not wish to discuss it here. . . . As my speculations have made me for a time not so sociable as is serviceable and useful for me, and as my spirits are somewhat exhausted, I have taken refuge for a short time in the study of poetry that I might be somewhat recreated by it. . . . Your great kindness and your favor, of which I have had so many proofs, make me believe that your advice and your letters will induce my father to be so favorable towards me as to send me the funds which are necessary for a young man, and which will infuse into me new spirit for the prosecution of my studies. Believe me, I desire and strive to be an honor to my father's house and yours.[26]

Sometime in 1713, Swedenborg left England for Holland. He arrived there at a time when peace negotiations were in progress between England, France, and Holland. As a rule Swedenborg was not much interested in politics or diplomacy, but this was a critical time for Sweden, because King Charles XII was in exile in Turkey. Like all patriotic Swedes, Swedenborg hoped that the peace negotiations between England, France, and Holland would branch into a larger settlement that would include Sweden, Poland, and Russia. He visited the site of the negotiations and met with some of the Swedish diplomats. But Swedenborg's hopes, and those of his fellow Swedes, were dashed. When the conference concluded, the warring powers signed the Peace of Utrecht, which ended the War of the Spanish Succession among the Western European powers (to learn more about this conflict, simply enter the keywords "war of Spanish succession" into any Internet search engine and browse the many sites listed). Unfortunately, the Great Northern War between Sweden and its neighbors continued to rage on until 1721.

From Holland, Swedenborg traveled to Paris. He arrived there early in 1714. He was impressed with the architecture of the city, particularly the palace of Versailles. He commented little, however, about the scientific progress of France, seeming to prefer the English and Dutch approach to science. During this time, Swedenborg put the finishing touches on a list of inventions he hoped to make in the near future. The list, which he sent home to Sweden, still exists. The list includes, among other things, the following inventions:

- The construction of a ship which, with its one-man crew, could go under the sea, in any desired direction, and could inflict much injury on enemy ships

- On constructions [locks] even in places where there is no flow of water, whereby a whole ship with its cargo can be raised to a given height in one or two hours

- A drawbridge which can be closed and opened from within the gates and walls

- A universal musical instrument whereby the most inexperienced player can produce all kinds of melodies, these being found marked on paper and in notes

- A water clock with water as the indicator which, by its flow, shows all the movable bodies in the heavens and produces other ingenious effects

- Item. A flying carriage, or the possibility of staying in the air and of being carried through it[27]

Some of these items quite accurately describe future inventions like the submarine, the airplane, a system of hydro-locks, and an automatic piano. Clearly, Swedenborg harbored desires of becoming the world's next Leonardo da Vinci. In time, some claimed that he achieved this distinction.

RETURN HOME

First, though, he had to reach home. He had been away for more than three years now, the plague was a thing of the past, and he longed to see Sweden again. Swedenborg traveled overland to the port of Rostock, Germany, where he spent several months. Just before leaving on a ship for Stockholm, he composed a poem in honor of King Charles XII:

> Ah, soon return, oh monarch of our love!
> Oh Sun of Sweden, waste not all thy light
> To illumine the crescent of the Ottomans:
> Thine absence we bewail, wandering in glooms
> Of midnight sorrow, save that these bright stars,
> That lead us on to victory, still console
> Thy people's hearts and bid them not despair.[28]

Remarkably, King Charles was then on his way home as well. After his almost five years exiled in Turkey, he arrived in the beleaguered city of Stralsund on October 31, 1714. The fates of the two returning Swedes were about to intersect.

The Mature
Man of Science

I find that young Swedenborg is a ready mathematician,
and possesses much aptitude for the mechanical sciences.

—Inventor Christopher Polhem

When Swedenborg and King Charles XII returned, the country was exhausted after 15 years of continuous warfare. The king still had the ability to excite and motivate his soldiers, but the population at large was another matter. The Swedish people wanted peace.

SWEDENBORG AND THE KING

Peace was the one thing King Charles would not give them. He came back from Turkey full of ambitious ideas and plans. His five years in foreign exile had not changed him one bit; it is little wonder that the Turks called him "Iron Head."

Swedenborg came home in the spring of 1715. He went straight to his father's estate at Brusbo, where he spent the next several months. Bishop Svedberg was pleased to see his son again, but urged him to consider a career in the diplomatic service. Swedenborg explained that he intended to continue his work in the realm of science.

Bishop Svedberg did his best to find a place for Emanuel. He wrote long letters to Swedish officials and finally sent one to King Charles himself. Reminding King Charles that he had long been a confidant of the monarch's father, Bishop Svedberg pleaded his son's case:

> May it please your Excellency—My son Emanuel, after five years' foreign travel, has at length returned home. I hope he may be found available for some Academy. He is accomplished in Oriental languages, as well as European, but especially he is an adept in poetry and mathematics. . . . If there should be an opening at an Academy here in Sweden, will your Excellency be so kind as advance him to fill it? With God's help he will honor his place.[29]

There was no answer from the king. He was far too busy putting together an army and hurrying to meet the next assault from Sweden's neighbors.

Swedenborg spent an uneventful summer at his father's house. He was frustrated to find that the drawings he had made of his potential new inventions had been misplaced. The written instructions survived, but Swedenborg did not want to spend a great deal of time remaking the illustrations. He wrote to his brother-in-law:

> I looked very carefully for the machines which I some time ago sent to my father; they were eight in number, but I was unable to discover the place in which he had laid them aside. He thinks they have been sent to you, which I hope with all my heart. . . . First, three drawings and plans for water-pumps, by which a large quantity of water can be raised in a short time from any sea or lake you choose. Second, two machines for raising weights by means of water, as easily and quickly as is done by mechanical forces. Third, some kinds of sluices, which can be constructed where there is no fall of water, and which will raise boats over hills, sand-banks, etc. Fourth, a machine to discharge by air ten or eleven thousand shots per hour. All these machines are carefully described and calculated algebraically. . . . Whatever additional success I may have in my designs, I will first communicate to you.[30]

This letter suggests an incredible audacity on Swedenborg's part. He believed he could put together all these machines and do so practically single-handedly. Once he even wrote to his brother-in-law suggesting that the professors at the University of Uppsala each voluntarily yield one-seventh of their salary to fund a new position there for himself! Eric Benzelius did all he could to suppress this ridiculous and pompous idea. It was also thanks to Benzelius that Swedenborg was introduced to Sweden's greatest scientist, Christopher Polhem.

THE NORTHERN INVENTOR
Born around 1662, Polhem had had a much tougher time in life

than Swedenborg. The Polhem family was Austrian, and some of Polhem's ancestors had been prominent noblemen in the Holy Roman Empire. The Polhems had moved north in pursuit of religious freedom, and Christopher Polhem was born in Visby, Sweden.[31] Polhem attended the University of Uppsala about 20 years earlier than Swedenborg. There, he had first shown his mechanical genius by working on the astronomical clock in the cathedral (Swedenborg would have remembered stories about this from his student days at Uppsala).[32] Polhem then went into mining research and became an inventor in his spare time. Thus, he and Swedenborg had several things in common, although Polhem had had to make his own way in life while Swedenborg had led a sheltered, some might even say a charmed, existence.

Polhem did his best to ingratiate himself with King Charles XII. Even during the king's years in Turkish exile, Polhem sent the Swedish monarch numerous drawings, descriptions, and ideas for new inventions; not surprisingly, the king was most interested in those that had military applications. By the time King Charles returned to Sweden in 1715, Polhem was the nation's most renowned scientist, the only one who could do much for another inventor—Emanuel Swedenborg.

Polhem wrote to Eric Benzelius about Swedenborg in December of 1715:

> I find that young Swedenborg is a ready mathematician, and possesses much aptitude for the mechanical sciences; and, if he continues as he has begun, he will in course of time be able to be of greater use to the King and to his country in this than in anything else.[33]

Swedenborg now used all the methods of flattery and persuasion he had absorbed through a lifetime of floating about in high society. He impressed Polhem with his idea for the publication of a new scientific magazine, Sweden's first, and flattered him by naming it *The Northern Inventor* (*Daedalus Hyperboreus*) in Polhem's honor. Each issue of the magazine would feature at least one of Polhem's inventions, and the overall thrust would be to promote scientific advancement in the homeland.

Polhem, naturally, was pleased to be honored in this fashion. He and Swedenborg launched the first edition of *The Northern Inventor* in 1716. One year later, in the fourth issue, Swedenborg was bold enough to propose something he had first put in a letter to his brother-in-law: a plan for a device that could fly. The article argued in favor of making a flying machine:

> But if we follow living nature, examining the proportions that the wing of a bird holds to its body, a similar mechanism might be invented, which should give us hope to be able to follow the bird in the air. First, let a car or boat or some object be made of light material such as cork or birch bark, with a room within for the operator. Second, in front as well as behind or all around, set a widely stretched sail parallel to the machine, forming within a hollow, or bend, which could be reefed like the sails of a ship. Third, place wings on the sides, to be worked up and down by a spiral spring, these wings also to be hollow below in order to increase the force and velocity.[34]

In a world where humans have left the atmosphere and ventured to the moon, this does not seem so extraordinary, but Swedenborg wrote this in 1716. The design was not made in his lifetime, but later generations of Swedes built a model of what the Swedenborg airplane would have been like. One of these replicas greets visitors to the Early Flight section of the Smithsonian Museum in Washington, D.C., today.[35]

Swedenborg found no one to take on this audacious project in his own lifetime. He was continually finding new avenues of thought and invention, but it seemed as if the Swedes of his day, with a few rare exceptions, could not keep up with him.

Christopher Polhem and Swedenborg now became colleagues, and Polhem soon brought Swedenborg before King Charles XII. Swedenborg later described the meeting:

> When Polhem received the King's orders to repair to Lund, he engaged me to go with him. Having been presented to his Majesty, he often did us the honor of conversing on the different branches of mathematics, and particularly on mechanics, the mode of calculating forces and other problems in mixed mathematics. He seemed to take great pleasure in these conversations, and often put questions as if he wished some easy information, but we soon found he knew more than we thought. [36]

The king proved to be especially interested in numbers:

> Conversing one day about arithmetic, his Majesty observed that the denary [decimal; proceeding by tens] arithmetic in universal use was most probably derived from counting on the fingers by illiterate people of old, who, when they had run through the fingers of both hands, repeated the process over and over again, keeping a tally of 10s. . . . The King was of opinion that, had such not been the origin of our mode of counting, a much better method might have been devised . . . . [37]

Neither Polhem nor Swedenborg was actually eager to reform the numerical system, but they made an appearance of doing so while they actually found other ways to serve King Charles. One of these was the long-dreamed-of canal between the east and west coasts of Sweden. Such a canal would allow Swedish ships to navigate between the Baltic and North Seas without having to pass by Danish ports. King Charles put the two men to this task, and they drew up extensive plans. The plans were not realized during Swedenborg's life due to a shortage of time and money, but Sweden finally completed the Trollhattan Locks in 1918.

Sometime in 1717, King Charles appointed Swedenborg extraordinary assessor of the Bureau of Mines.[38] This was one of the most important bureaucratic councils in the nation, and the appointment of such a young man to the post was bound to cause some jealousy. Swedenborg accepted it gladly even though he knew that as an "extraordinary" assessor he would not receive any pay until the time when he became a "regular" assessor.

Clearly, Swedenborg was now a man on the move. He had won the favor of King Charles, and he was now seen as one of the more important of Sweden's scientists. Swedenborg knew he had to keep working to stay in the king's good graces, and he regularly brought editions of *The Northern Inventor* to show the king.

Meanwhile, there was talk of marriage. Christopher Polhem had five children, three of whom were daughters. One of these, by the name of Ermina, was suggested to Swedenborg as a wife. Swedenborg neither jumped at the prospect nor shrank from it. Instead, he continued to meet the girl to see if she met his hopes. Eventually, he decided that she did, and he asked Polhem's permission to marry her.

Christopher Polhem was quite willing, but his daughter was not. When Swedenborg learned that she greatly loved someone else and that she had burned the marriage papers that would unite her with Swedenborg, he quickly broke off all discussion of marriage. It is impossible to say whether this matter was a factor, but Swedenborg's relations with Polhem began to cool at around the same time. In addition to the awkwardness of the broken engagement, the older man may have felt threatened by Swedenborg's genius and scientific output.

Swedenborg suffered another stroke of bad fortune when King Charles XII was killed at the siege of Frederickshall in November 1718.[39] With King Charles dead, and his relationship with Christopher Polhem no longer as friendly, Swedenborg suddenly found himself with few patrons and fewer options.

Sweden, too, was going through a sea of change. The throne passed to Charles's younger sister, who became Queen Ulrika

Eleanora. Swedish historians generally consider 1718 to be a turning point in their nation's history; they have labeled the period between 1718 and 1772 the "Era of Freedom." During this time, the Swedish nobles and deliberative bodies took on a greater role in politics, and the idea of absolute government by the monarch appeared to have been abandoned.

There were some people who protested the change. Bishop Jesper Svedberg, who was in semi-retirement and could easily have stayed out of the matter, rose to give a speech against the new constitutional government:

> I stood up and declared the opinion of the Clergy with well-chosen words, approximately, we have no permit to take from the ruler the power that God in His Words has ascribed to him . . . the King stands in God's place on earth. His power is of God. If he abuses it, so he shall answer before God, and not before his subjects. Here we have no Polish Republic, or some kind of English government. We have the power of a King, set out in the Royal Chapter of our old Law Book.[40]

These were the words of the old Swedish bishop. They did not reflect the opinion of his still youthful son.

The Great Change

*Every one, from the light of reason, may see that
nature, conforming to principles of geometry,
is ever pursuing a most simple course, a course
peculiar to herself, and truly mechanical.*

—Emanuel Swedenborg, *First Principles of Natural Things*

Emanuel Swedenborg did not grieve deeply over the death of King Charles XII. The relationship, for both men, had been one of convenience, and Swedenborg was, in general, opposed to war for its own sake. Like many other Swedes, he believed that the king had gone too far in pursuing war and that Sweden had suffered as a result.

ENNOBLEMENT

One rather important change occurred almost immediately. Soon after she took the throne, Queen Eleanora ennobled all the living children of Bishop Jesper Svedberg. The bishop had been asking for this honor for many years. He knew that as a bishop he could not be ennobled, but he wanted the designation for his children. As the oldest surviving son, Emanuel became Baron Swedenborg in 1718.[41]

One year later, Swedenborg's stepmother died. He had been her favorite stepchild, and she left him the bulk of her share of the family mining property. This allowed him a comfortable, though not extravagant, income, freeing him to pursue his interests. This was just as well, since his fellow assessors on the Board of Mines prevented him from receiving his full salary for that post until 1727.

With his new title as Baron Swedenborg came a seat in the House of Nobles (*Riddarhurst*), one of the four houses of Sweden's Parliament. We do not know for certain how important this was to Swedenborg, but his position in the House of Nobles meant a great deal to his father. Jesper Svedberg had now seen the culmination of many of his ambitions for the family.

Emanuel Swedenborg now held two posts. He was both an extraordinary assessor for the Board of Mines and a member of the House of Nobles. He paid due attention to both tasks, giving many hours to the study of improvement of the mines. Mining was in Swedenborg's blood, and he went for long horseback rides through rather grim countryside, seeking new and better locations for mines. He also attended the meetings of the House of Nobles on a regular basis, although he did not speak very often. The slight speech impediment he had suffered his whole life made him reluctant to deliver addresses, but he did write long memorials that were read aloud by secretaries.

Altogether, one could say that by the age of 30, Swedenborg was a very successful man. Whether he was happy or fulfilled is less obvious.

There is no sign of unhappiness in Swedenborg's letters. Rather, there is the sense that he wanted to move on to something more important. He now wanted to achieve something great in the scientific realm. He came close with *Motion and Position of the Earth and Planets,* which was published in 1719. Swedenborg presented fossils as evidence that most of Sweden had once been under water.[42] Today, we consider this a very likely proposition. We know that the Earth has changed numerous times in its six billion years of existence. Swedenborg, however, wrote in a time when many people still believed that Earth was only about 6,000 years old. Given such a short time frame, it seemed impossible that Sweden, with its rocky coastlines and severe mountains, had once been under water.

Swedenborg paid for the costs of the publication out of his own pocket. This would, unfortunately, be a trend that would last most of his life. He was so interested in obscure matters of science (and later in religion) that he had a very small market of potential book buyers.

A letter to his brother-in-law, written late in 1719, revealed some of Swedenborg's frustration and impatience:

> This is the last time that I will publish myself, because every-day and home affairs grow of small account, and because I have already worked myself poor by them. I have been singing long enough [for my supper]; let us see whether any one will come forward and hand me some bread in return.[43]

JOURNEYS IN EUROPE

Swedenborg went abroad in the spring of 1720. He hoped to find other scientists and philosophers who were less competitive and jealous than those he knew in Sweden. Years later, he described his travels:

> I again went abroad, going to Holland by Copenhagen and Hamburg. There I published my *Prodromus Principiorum Rerum Naturalium*, and several other short treatises in octavo. From Holland I traveled to Aix-la-Chapelle, Leige, Cologne, and other adjacent places, examining the mines there. Thence I went to Leipsic, where I published my *Miscellenea Observata*. Leaving that town I visited all the mines in Saxony, and then returned to Hamburg. From Hamburg I returned to Brunswick and Goslar, and visited all the mines in the Harz Mountains belonging to the houses of Hanover and Luneburg. The father-in-law of a son of the Emperor and of a son of the Czar, Duke Louis Rudolph, who resided at Blankenburg, graciously defrayed all my expenses.[44]

Was this really possible? Did hospitality between nobles of different countries reach to this extent of generosity? They did when the visitor was a member of the major nobility or if there was a strong familial connection. Swedenborg, however, was neither of the high nobility nor a relative. Perhaps a German noble agreed to finance his visit because he was impressed by Swedenborg as a man of science. Then again, Swedenborg may have performed investigations of the mines in return for his bed and board.

Swedenborg returned home in the summer of 1722. He quickly addressed a letter to King Frederic, the German husband of Queen Ulrika Eleanora:

> I therefore venture in all humility to come before you with some measures by which the mode of working the mines in Sweden may be improved, limiting myself for the present to

some improvements in the working of copper. For, by carefully investigating the process used in Sweden, and comparing
it with that employed abroad, taking into consideration the
difference in the ore, I have discovered some means by which
the yield of copper may be considerably increased.[45]

Nothing came of the matter. Either the king was not interested
or the letter became entangled in the long line of Swedish
bureaucrats. It is no wonder that Swedenborg despaired of the
state of genuine scientific inquiry.

For the next 10 years, Swedenborg labored on what he
believed would be his greatest contribution to science. By the
spring of 1733, he was ready to travel to Germany and Holland
to publish his masterwork.

THE SCIENTIFIC MASTERPIECE

Swedenborg's *Philosophical and Mineralogical Works* (*Opera
Philosophica et Mineralia*) is a massive three-volume work. The
first volume was *First Principles of Natural Things* (*Principia
Rerum Naturalium*). Here, we find Swedenborg's scientific beliefs,
at the mature age of 45:

> Every one, from the light of reason, may see that nature,
> conforming to principles of geometry, is ever pursuing a
> most simple course, a course peculiar to herself, and truly
> mechanical. He may likewise see that all things in the world
> arise from what is uncompounded, and therefore from a
> single fountain-head and a primitive cause; that this primitive
> cause enters into the various things that are caused (a truth
> which necessarily follows, if further entities are to be derived
> from those which have already been brought into existence);
> also that there could have been no other cause than the one
> which had proceeded by descent, as it were, from its first
> patent or simple.[46]

This seemed rather likely to people of the eighteenth century, and it did not diverge from the beliefs of the Church. Swedenborg was on safe ground, so far. He went on:

> This cause, therefore, must be latent in the first simple; and there must enter a similar cause into the first entity derived from it. Now since the world deduces its origin and subsequent increments, by means of a connected contiguous series, from the primary or single end through intermediates to another end; and since there must be present a cause, and indeed an efficient and active cause, before anything can be produced in a series; it follows that there must be a passive, an active, and as a product from both, a compound, or elementary.[47]

This proposition was a little more difficult. Was Swedenborg making a sly allusion to what would later be called evolution?

> If therefore there is anything of a composite kind, it must consist of two principles, a passive and an active; without these nature herself would be, as it were, in a state of celibacy, destitute of progeny, without a derived entity, without any new efficient, without effect, without series, without phenomena; in a word, without worlds.[48]

This certainly followed from logic, but it required the reader to accept Swedenborg's original statement that everything living proceeded from a first, or simple, cause. There followed hundreds of pages of natural philosophy or what might be called cosmology. Swedenborg laid out his view of the creation of the universe. He described what "original" man or "natural" man in the state of Adam must have been:

> To begin, then, with man in his state of integrity and complete perfection. In such a man we may conceive that there was such a complete contiguity throughout the parts of his system, that every motion proceeding with a free course from his grosser parts or principles could arrive, through an

uninterrupted connection, at his most subtle substance or
active principle . . . . Such a man may be compared to the
world itself, in which all things are contiguous from the sun
to the lowest part of our atmosphere. Thus the motions
about the sun, or rays, proceed with an uninterrupted
course, and almost instantaneously, by means of contiguity,
through the more subtle or the grosser elements, through
ether to air, till they reach the eye and act upon it, by virtue
of such connection, as if they were present.[49]

This was the state of Original Man, Swedenborg declared.
Because there were no blocks to his perception, he received
knowledge and even wisdom automatically. This wonderful
time, alas, had long since disappeared.

Humans live instead in a world in which they must acquire all
knowledge and all wisdom through experience. This does not
come easily, even for the best mind or heart. Swedenborg was
now following in the tradition of John Locke, who had described
man at birth as a *tabula rasa* (the Latin phrase means "blank
slate") upon which experience writes its book of knowledge.
Swedenborg, more optimistic than Locke, however, believed that
people could acquire all they needed; he held out the hope that
the state of Original Man, as experienced by the biblical Adam,
would someday return.

Swedenborg also held out the possibility, even the likelihood,
that life existed on other planets. He hinted that the universe was
in a continual state of creation:

> She [Nature] is most fertile and equally ambitious; for she
> is never at rest, but always desirous to advance and to
> extend the bounds of her dominion; indeed the more fertile
> she is, the greater are her efforts. She extends her forces and
> her sway into infinity, in which there are neither boundaries
> nor ends, and where she may continue to multiply without
> end. . . . Hence new heavens one after the other may arise;
> in these heavens, new vortices and world-systems; in these

world-systems, new planets; around the planets, new satellites; and in this manner, at the will of the Deity, new creations may arise in endless succession.[50]

In 1733, Swedenborg went to Leipzig, Germany, to oversee the printing of his *Principia*. During his 12 months in Europe, Swedenborg enjoyed life to the hilt. He was now a prominent natural philosopher as well as a Swedish baron. Life appeared to have come full circle for the ambitious scientist.

DREAMS
Jesper Svedberg died in 1735, one year after the publication of *First Principles of Natural Things*. The old bishop had

THE UNCONSCIOUS ACCORDING TO FREUD AND JUNG

Both Sigmund Freud and Carl Jung were pioneers in the study of the unconscious. According to both men (and described in the earlier writings of Swedenborg), the unconscious is a great floating mass of memory, feeling, and emotional subjectivity. This great mass directs much of our thoughts, actions, and beliefs, even when we are indeed unconscious of its presence.

Freud called dreams the "royal road to the unconscious." Jung believed the same thing, but the two men diverged when it came to interpretation. Freud described the unconscious as very personal, closely tied to the repressed feelings of the individual person (he also harped on sexual repression as a major cause of anxiety and discontent). Jung had a much broader approach. He described the unconscious as the repository of the thoughts, feelings, and beliefs of entire cultures or of the world as a whole. This is called the collective unconscious. Jung agreed with Freud that sexuality was important but believed that all forms of expression and communication, sexuality included, were of vital importance to humans.

Between them, Freud and Jung changed our present-day appreciation of ourselves as human beings. Of the two, Jung was more aware of Swedenborg and made reference to Swedenborg as one of the earliest pioneers of the unconscious mind.

certainly done well in life. He had married several times and had raised nine children. He had become something of a legend in his time, and he was given a magnificent funeral, with a section of the cathedral at Varnhem Cloister set aside as his final resting place.[51]

Swedenborg was hard at work on another book. His *Economy of the Animal Kingdom*, was published in 1741.

Numerous scholars have noted that this was a poor, inaccurate title for the book. A better one might have been *The Human Body and its Relation to the Soul*. In it, Swedenborg was delving deeper than ever into the workings of the body, and he was simultaneously looking for what he hoped would be the first scientific look at the soul.

Swedenborg began with the premise that human beings have a soul. Since many other aspects of human life, like the brain, heart, and arteries, were coming under scientific surveillance, why not the soul as well? We have to remember that the divisions between science (which was often called natural philosophy), psychology, and philosophy were less strictly defined in the eighteenth century than is now the case.

Swedenborg began his discussions on the body and the soul with the blood:

> The animal kingdom, the economy of which I am about to consider anatomically, physically, and philosophically, regards the blood as its common fountain and general principle. In undertaking, therefore, to treat of this economy, the doctrine of the blood must be the first propounded, although it is the last that is capable of being brought to completion.[52]

The circulation of the blood had been shown as early as 1628 with the publication of William Harvey's magnificent work on the subject. Swedenborg pointed out that the blood was the fountain of everything else, and, therefore, everything else had to be examined in order to understand how the entire chain worked.

Swedenborg quoted from numerous earlier authors to support his arguments. About 30 pages into the book, he laid bare one of his key hypotheses:

> There is a certain fluid, of the highest degree of purity, called by some the animal spirit, which enters into the red blood as its principal substance, and which constitutes its vital essence. . . . *First*, it is shown, that such a spirituous fluid as we have just mentioned, is interiorly conceived in the cortical and cineritious substance of the brain, the medulla oblongata and medulla spinalis; that it is next emitted into all the medullary fibres or origins of the nerves, and is thence ultimately derived into the blood.[53]

It is not clear whether Swedenborg did much dissection himself, or if he relied on the writings of famous anatomists. Whichever is the case, he proceeded to lay out some very new and controversial theories, some of which have been confirmed by twentieth-century science. He wrote, for example:

> I intend to examine physically and philosophically, the whole anatomy of the body, its viscera, abdominal and thoracic, the generative organs of both sexes, and the organs of the five senses. Likewise, the anatomy of all parts of the cerebrum, cerebellum, medulla oblongata, and medulla spinalis. . . . The Learned in general, and the Anatomists in particular, describe the Animal Spirits as running through the finest threads of the Nerves, as calling out the force of the muscles, as being sublimated from the blood, and as having their birth in the brain, which they term the mart and emporium of the animal spirits.[54]

Swedenborg had a great deal more to say about blood: "The lungs may be considered as a single stomach consisting of an infinite number of smaller ones, feeding on aerial food, just as the stomach feeds on terrestrial food." He continued:

> We thus have three fountains for the three Bloods: the Brain for the Animal Spirits, the Lungs for the White Blood, and the Heart for the Red. The motion of the Red Blood is Rotatory, of the White Spiral, and of the Animal Spirits Vortical.[55]

Most important was Swedenborg's discussion of the cerebral cortex. As he discussed in *The Economy of the Animal Kingdom*, numerous earlier authors had described the cortex, but none had assigned to it the same importance as Swedenborg:

> We infer that the cortex is the principal substance of the brain; situated in the very first term of the fibres and the last of the arteries: consequently in the middle, in order that it may be able to extract from the blood the purer essences and animal spirits, and transmit them immediately into the finest medullary filaments, and so into the nervous filaments of the body.[56]

Swedenborg did not only intuit; he used both inductive and deductive reasoning to reach his point. His deductive reasoning came from the works of the anatomists who preceded him; his inductive reasoning came from his belief that everything in nature is connected and is in continuous motion. Therefore, it would make no sense to have a cortex with such fibers if it was not designed to send the fluid around the body. Just a few paragraphs later, he made another strong statement, which was later verified by modern science:

> We may thus understand the course of the circulation of the animal spirits; namely, that it is from the cortex into the universal fibres, from the fibres into the blood, from the blood into the brain, and so back into the cortex, whereby no portion of these spirits perishes without use. We may also understand

the moments of this circulation; namely, that they are synchronous with those of the respiration of the lungs, which wonderfully concur in promoting and transfusing this truly animal juice through the nerves.[57]

Some of Swedenborg's words sound archaic to us. Modern science does not use terms like "animal spirits" or "spirituous fluid." In spite of the differences in language, modern science, since 1910 or so, has confirmed some of Swedenborg's findings. The cerebral cortex is the seat for the commands sent to the limbs of the body to put the body in motion. Swedenborg also came very close to hitting upon the endocrine glands as part of the "humoral" changes that occur in men and women.

How he did all this remains one of the great questions about Swedenborg's life. We know, from his diary, that he went to operas and concerts, and that he enjoyed parties and balls as much as any man of his time. Somehow, in the wee hours of the morning perhaps, Swedenborg also found the time and the intellectual will to discover some things that would not be verified for over a century. One of the tragic aspects of Swedenborg's scientific career is that he was often so far ahead of his contemporaries that they took little note of him or his work. His *On the Brain* (*De Cerebro*) would not be discovered and published until the late nineteenth century.

Swedenborg arrived in Holland toward the end of 1743. In chapter one we saw that Swedenborg underwent a profound spiritual change in early April of 1744, which was Easter-time. Just a few hours after the dream which was discussed in chapter one, Swedenborg had more dreams, ones which centered around two very important "father figures" in his life: his natural father, Bishop Svedberg, and King Charles XII:

I then saw my father dressed in another costume, almost reddish. He asked me to come, and he took me by the arms, which were in half-sleeves, but with detectable cuffs in front.

He took both the cuffs and tied them with my bands. That I was wearing cuffs meant that I did not belong to the clergy but am, and should be, a civil servant. Then he asked for my opinion about a certain question, that a king has permitted some thirty ordained clergy to marry, thus changing their state [in life]. I replied that I have written something about such matters, but it has no bearing on this.[58]

Swedenborg and his father had never been close while the bishop was alive. Bishop Svedberg had been too pompous, too concerned with his worldly "estate" to be much concerned with his son the scientist. But this dream shows that Swedenborg was about to reconcile his father's spiritual past with his own spiritual future. The words, "I am, and should be, a civil servant" indicate that Swedenborg had broken through an old inhibition: his fear that he was not good enough for his earthly father. Just as his heavenly father had appeared in his first religious dream (see chapter one) and said "Well then, do!" so now, Bishop Svedberg, the earthly father, was giving full permission to Swedenborg to carry out his mission in the way that suited him, as a civil servant.

Other dreams followed, with Bishop Svedberg and King Charles XII being the people who most often appeared. Swedenborg was clearly in the midst of what we today would call a psychological breakthrough. When he returned to Sweden a year later, Swedenborg would be different indeed: a man who had confronted his deepest fears and emerged with confirmation concerning his earthly work.

6

Heavenly Secrets

He spoke to me and asked if I have a health certificate;
and to this I replied, "Lord, thou knowest better
than I." He said, "Well then, do!"

—Emanuel Swedenborg, describing
one of his mystical experiences

wedenborg returned home a changed man. The changes were internal and subtle. He did not advertise that he had gone through a spiritual transformation but rather hinted at it through his actions. First, he resigned from his position in the Bureau of Mines. This had been one of the mainstays of his life for 25 years, and he let it go with surprising ease.

Swedenborg lived comfortably in his home near the water in Stockholm. He was not rich, but the two inheritances from his mother and his stepmother had made him an independent man. Now he intended to use that independence and the time it afforded him to spread the word of God.

Swedenborg kept his position in the House of Nobles. As a baron, he could not do otherwise, but he had never been a speaker in the House, and his duties there did not require a great deal of energy. He was therefore free to plunge into one of the greatest of all his literary projects, the *Heavenly Secrets* (*Arcana Caelestia*).

THE SPIRITUAL MASTERPIECE

Swedenborg labored on *Heavenly Secrets* for year after year. His outward appearance gave little indication of the work he was doing; his neighbors viewed him as a kindly gentleman, more interested in his flower garden than in worldly affairs. Little did they suspect that his interests had grown to include "otherworldly" matters.

Heavenly Secrets was published in London between 1749 and 1756. The work grew to a total of eight massive volumes that were published in successive order. Swedenborg's publisher, John Lewis, had high hopes for each volume. His advertisement began:

> This work is intended to be such an exposition of the whole
> Bible as was never attempted in any language before. The
> author is a learned foreigner, who wrote and printed the first
> volume of the same work but last year, all in Latin, which may
> be seen at my shop in Paternoster-Row. [59]

Only over the past two and a half centuries has *Heavenly Secrets* been examined at length. Its volumes are dense, rich, confusing, and enlightening all at once. To begin with, Swedenborg announced his belief in the doctrine of correspondences:

> From the mere letter of the Word of the Old Testament no one would ever see that this part of the Word contains heavenly arcane, and that everything within it both in general and in particular has reference to the Lord, to His heaven, and to

SWEDENBORG'S PUBLISHERS

The expression "publisher" was hardly used at the time that Swedenborg wrote; publishers were known as "printers." The art of printing through the use of movable type had been around for about 300 years, but many of the methods remained the same as they had been in the time of Johann Gutenberg.

Swedenborg' earliest papers were published in Skara, Uppsala, or Stockholm. Almost all of his works were written in Latin, which made his audience rather small. One of the major and surprising features of *The Northern Inventor* is that it was written and printed in Swedish.

Later, as his scientific fame grew, Swedenborg went abroad regularly to oversee all aspects of the printing of his works. His *Principia* was printed in the German cities of Leipzig and Danzig in 1734, and his *Economy of the Animal Kingdom* was printed in Holland. Both works were in Latin.

Then he wrote the *Heavenly Secrets* and *Heaven and Its Wonders and Hell*. Both were printed abroad. *Heavenly Secrets* was printed in English and sold in London. By now, Swedenborg had strayed from writing about science, and he could no longer expect the support of his previous publishers.

Toward the end of his life, Swedenborg was accused, in a general way, of heresy against the Swedish Lutheran Church. Swedish King Adolphus decreed that no additional Swedenborgian books should be brought into Sweden, but he also noted that since the previous ones had been written in Latin, a language only the educated few could read, there was little harm in them. One can only wonder what might have happened had Swedenborg published more in Sweden and in the Swedish language.

the church, to faith, and to all things connected therewith: for from the letter or sense of the letter all that any one can see is that—to speak generally—everything therein has reference to the external rites of the Jewish Church. [60]

Though he did not employ the word "correspondences" yet, Swedenborg meant that everything in the Old and New Testaments was written in a code, as it were, and that every word, every letter, indeed, every comma or colon in the Scriptures bore some *correspondence* to the life of God and the heavens. Swedenborg saw himself as uniquely qualified to penetrate the coded meaning in the Bible, and he was about to lay the results before his readers.

Swedenborg had never suffered from false modesty. We must remember that at the age of 28 he had suggested that all the professors at Uppsala University take pay cuts so that a new position might be created for him. He was now well advanced in years and no longer exhibited the brash qualities of his youth, but he was more than ever convinced of the power of his intellect. This, joined with the spiritual reformation he had undergone, would enable him to spread the word of God to the masses.

He went on to explain that:

The Christian world, however, is as yet profoundly ignorant of the fact that all things in the Word both in general and in particular, indeed, the very smallest particulars down to the least iota, signify and enfold within them spiritual and heavenly things; and for this reason the Old Testament is but little cared for. [61]

Swedenborg was correct. Men and women of science had been discounting the Old Testament for some time. Swedenborg's own work had, in some way, reflected this trend. His geological discoveries and his publication of fossil items, 30 years earlier, had been another piece of the puzzle that indicated that the world was far more than 6,000 years old. Now, however, he was emerging as the prophet of new times, one who required that his followers examine the book as they had done in older times:

> Yet that the Word is really of this character might be known from the single consideration that, being the Lord's and from the Lord, it could not possibly be given unless it contained within it such things as belong to heaven, to the church, and to faith.[62]

When Swedenborg wrote "the church," he did not mean the Swedish Lutheran Church of his father. Still less did he mean the Roman Catholic Church, for which he maintained a lifelong dislike. Swedenborg defined four ages of "the church" that he had in mind: the Most Ancient, then the Ancient, then the Jewish, and finally, the Christian.

Swedenborg's discussion began with the Most Ancient Church, which dated to the time of Adam and Eve:

> In the most ancient time mankind was distinguished into houses, families, and nations; a house consisting of the husband and wife with their children, together with some of their family who served; a family of a greater or smaller number of houses, that lived not far apart and yet not together; and a nation, of a larger or smaller number of families. The reason why they dwelt thus alone by themselves, distinguished only into houses, families, and nations, was that by this means the church might be preserved entire, that all the houses and families might be dependent on their parent, and thereby remain in love and true worship. . . . Thus the church was a living representative of the kingdom of the Lord; for in the Lord's kingdom there are innumerable societies, each one distinct from every other, according to the differences of love and faith. This, as observed above, is what is meant by "living alone," and by "dwelling in tents."[63]

Swedenborg described the time of the Most Ancient Church as the greatest in human memory. Men and women dwelt together in peace, and there was little need for verbal communication since people could read each other's thoughts merely by glancing at each other's faces. There was no deception, and nothing was kept secret.

This wonderful time did not endure. By the time of Noah, in the Old Testament, a transition had been made from the Most Ancient Church to the Ancient one:

> By "Noah" is signified a new church, which is to be called the Ancient Church, for the sake of distinction between the Most Ancient Church, which was before the flood, and that which was after the flood. The states of these two churches were entirely different. The state of the Most Ancient Church was such that they had from the Lord a perception of good and the derivative truth. The state of the Ancient Church, or "Noah," became such that they had a conscience of good and truth. Such as is the difference between having perception and having conscience, such was the difference of state of the Most Ancient and the Ancient Church. Perception is not conscience; the celestial have perception; the spiritual have conscience. The Most Ancient Church was celestial; the Ancient was spiritual.[64]

As Swedenborg employed the terms "perception" and "conscience," they meant the difference between knowing and acting upon truth and believing and testifying to truth. The former state, that of knowledge and action, is superior to that of belief and testifying to that belief. In this way, Swedenborg showed a decline from the Most Ancient Church to the Ancient Church.

Knowing that his readers would want to know some of the differences between earthly things and divine ones, Swedenborg wrote of differences in speech:

> The speech of spirits with man, as before said, is effected by words; but the speech of spirits among themselves is by ideas

wherein words originate, such are the ideas of thought; these, however, are not so obscure as are man's ideas while he lives in the body, but are distinct, like those of speech. Human thought, after the decease of the body, becomes more distinct and clear. . . . The speech of spirits is diverse: each society or family of spirits, and even every spirit, can be distinguished from others by their speech, just as is the case with men, not only by the affections which make the life of the speech . . . but also by the tones.[65]

The further one progresses into *Heavenly Secrets*, the more personal and subjective Swedenborg's descriptions become:

Much has been said about the visions of certain persons who have declared that they have seen many things, and who did them, but in fantasy. I have been instructed about them, and it was likewise shown how they take place. There are spirits who by means of fantasies induce appearances that seem to be real.[66]

Swedenborg went on to discriminate between fantasy spirits, enthusiastic spirits, good spirits, and genuine visions:

By genuine visions are meant visions or sights of such things in the other life as have real existence, and are nothing but actual things that can be seen by the eyes of the spirit and not by the eyes of the body, and that appear to a man when his interior sight is opened by the Lord.[67]

Swedenborg also had much to say about the Last Judgment:

By the Last Judgment is meant the last time of a church, and also the last state of each person's life. As regards the last time of the church, it was the Last Judgment of the Most Ancient Church, which was before the flood, when their posterity perished; whose destruction is described by the flood. . . .

The Last Judgment of the present church, which is called the
Christian Church, is what is meant by John in the Apocalypse
by the "New Heaven and the New Earth."[68]

It is also obvious that Swedenborg was clear about his belief
that another Day of Judgment was about to come:

That a Last Judgment is at hand, cannot be so evident on the
earth and within the church as in the other life, wither all souls
arrive and flock together. At this day the world of spirits is full
of evil genii and evil spirits, mostly from the Christian world,
among whom there reign nothing but hatreds, revenges,
cruelties, obscenities, and deceitful machinations.[69]

Why was Swedenborg so gloomy about the end of time? Had
he been the same man, the same experimental scientist, he had
been a decade earlier in 1740, Swedenborg might have been
delighted at the new possibilities for new advances in knowledge. He was now, however, a man of the spirit, and the times
seemed dark indeed.

SWEDENBORG'S GREATEST CRITIC

Heavenly Secrets did not find many buyers when it was first
published. Most educated readers, it seemed, were not ready
for Swedenborg's form of exposition. The book did, however,
capture the attention of one very important buyer: the German
philosopher Immanuel Kant. About a dozen years later, Kant
wrote a critique of the metaphilosophers in general and of
Swedenborg in particular. Kant's work was entitled *Dreams of a
Spirit-Seer Illustrated by Dreams of Metaphysics.* Kant began:

If we put all together, that the school-boy rehearses, that the
crowd relates, and that the philosopher demonstrated about
spirits, this would seem to constitute no small part of our
knowledge.... For we seldom hear at academies the comfortable and ofttimes reasonable "I do not know." Certain newer

philosophers, as they like to be called, overcome this question easily. A spirit, they say, is a being possessed of reason. Then it is no miracle to see spirits; for he who sees men, sees beings possessing reason.[70]

Kant explained that it was not his place either to put credence in Swedenborg's conversations with angels or to refuse any belief whatsoever. His point was to find a place on which reason could stand so that people could know whether their thoughts were of real things or false ones. As he put it:

> Every reasonable man will readily concede that here human intelligence has reached its limit. For while, by experience alone, we can perceived that things of this world which we call "material" possess such a force, we can never conceive of the reason why they exist.[71]

Through much of the book, Immanuel Kant addressed his remarks to metaphysicians in general. In the second chapter, entitled "A Dreamer's Ecstatic Journey through the World of Spirits," he took direct aim at Swedenborg:

> I come to the point, the works of my hero. If many authors who are now forgotten, or, at least in future will be without fame, deserve no small credit because, in the composition of big works, they took no heed of the expenditure of their reason, Mr. Swedenborg doubtless should carry highest honors among them all. For, surely, his bottle in the lunar world is quite full, and is inferior to none among all those which Ariosto has seen there, filled with the reason that was lost here, and which the owners one day will have to seek again; so utterly empty of the last drop of reason is his big work. . . . The big work of this author comprises eight volumes quarto full of nonsense.[72]

Thus was Swedenborg damned. Kant was the greatest German philosopher of his time (of any time, some would argue). His blanket condemnation of *Heavenly Secrets* meant that no German student took Swedenborg seriously for the next 100 years.

Ironically, Kant himself adopted and adapted some of Swedenborg's ideas just a few years later. It has been shown that Kant quoted from Swedenborg when he penned his illustrious *Dissertation on the Two Worlds* in 1770. In that work, Kant used some of Swedenborg's thinking as well as that of an earlier German philosopher, Gottfried Wilhelm Leibniz. Kant argued that all things are composed of earthly and knowable parts and spiritual and unknowable elements. This turnaround was too late for Swedenborg. His reputation had suffered a grievous blow from which it would not recover until the twentieth century.

7

Heaven
and Hell

*By the Last Judgment is meant the last time of a church,
and also the last state of each person's life.*

—Emanuel Swedenborg, *Heavenly Secrets*

In 1758, Swedenborg went abroad to publish a number of his books. The one of this group that is most remembered is *Heaven and Its Wonders and Hell*. This was Swedenborg's only theological work written for a broad audience, and it remains the one most read to this day.

THE DESCRIPTION OF HEAVEN AND HELL

Swedenborg started with his description of heaven. Like the scientist he had once been, he went into greater detail and analysis than is customary in theological works:

> As there are infinite varieties in heaven, and no one society nor any one angel is exactly like any other, there are in heaven general, specific, and particular divisions. The general division is into two kingdoms, the specific into three heavens, and the particular into innumerable societies.[73]

Swedenborg named the two divisions. Heaven was divided into the Celestial Kingdom and the Spiritual Kingdom. To readers today, these two words seem just about synonymous, but to Swedenborg there were important differences. First, the Celestial Kingdom was closest to God, and therefore the most interior. He described each of the kingdoms and separations as something like a large circle, radiating out from the inner center that was God:

> As the angels that constitute the celestial kingdom receive the Divine of the Lord more interiorly they are called interior or higher angels; and for the same reason the heavens that they constitute are called interior and higher heavens. They are called higher and lower, because these terms designate what is interior and what is exterior.[74]

Swedenborg claimed that the celestial angels, being closer to God, received his truth more readily:

> Such angels, as soon as they hear Divine truths, will and do them instead of storing them up in their memory and afterward considering whether they are true.[75]

This echoed one of Swedenborg's oldest and deepest beliefs: the importance of usefulness. These celestial angels were able to will and act immediately and were therefore more useful to God than were the spiritual angels. He emphasized a distinction between the two groups:

> Because of this difference between the angels of the celestial kingdom and the angels of the spiritual kingdom they are not together, and have no intercourse with each other. They are able to communicate only through intermediate angelic societies, which are called celestial-spiritual.[76]

Again, one is reminded of Swedenborg the scientist. The celestial-spiritual angels mediated between the two major groups of angels in the same kind of manner that the cerebral cortex sent out messages to the heart and limbs.

Swedenborg then described the three different heavens:

> There are three heavens, entirely distinct from each other, an inmost or third, a middle or second, and an outmost or first. These have the same order and relation to each other as the highest part of man, or his head, the middle part, or body, and the lowest, or feet; or as the upper, the middle, and the lower stories of a house.[77]

As with the angels, so, too, with the heavens:

> All perfection increases toward interiors and decreases toward exteriors, since interiors are nearer to the Divine, and are in themselves purer, while exteriors are more remote from the Divine, and are in themselves grosser.[78]

Then there were the innumerable societies. Angels might look a great deal alike, but each one was as unique as a snowflake. Swedenborg stressed the point, saying that he had spoken to angels about the possibility of two creations being exactly the same, and they had been horrified at the thought. It followed, therefore, that the angels were different and formed different societal groups. The more Swedenborg described the division of the heavens into three parts and the angels into different social groups, the more the heavens seemed to resemble life on Earth.

Swedenborg defined "correspondence" much more clearly in this book than he had done in *Heavenly Secrets*:

> The whole natural world corresponds to the spiritual world, and not merely the natural world in general, but also every particular of it; and as a consequence everything in the natural world that springs from the spiritual world is called a correspondent. It must be understood that the natural world springs from and has permanent existence from the spiritual world, precisely like an effect from its effecting cause. [79]

If Swedenborg seemed to be reverting to his scientific past, he invoked the sciences even more two pages later:

> The celestial kingdom corresponds in general to the heart and to all things of the heart in the whole body, and the spiritual kingdom to the lungs and to all things of the lungs in the whole body. Likewise in man heart and lungs form two kingdoms, the heart ruling through the arteries and veins, and the lungs through the tendinous and motor fibers, both together in every exertion and movement. [80]

Many readers, stopping here, might think that everything Swedenborg had to say was in the abstract. The second half of the book became much more explicit. Consider what he had to say about the experience immediately following death:

> I was reduced into a state of insensibility as to the bodily senses, thus almost into the state of dying persons, retaining however my interior life unimpaired . . . . that I might perceive and remember what happens to those who have died and are being resuscitated . . . . The angels who sat at my head were perfectly silent, merely communicating their thoughts by the face . . .

it was permitted me to perceive their cogitative speech. An aromatic odor was perceived, like that of an embalmed corpse, for when the celestial angels are present, the cadaverous odor is perceived as if it were aromatic, this when perceived by evil spirits prevents their approach. Meanwhile I perceived that the region of the heart was kept very closely united with the celestial angels, as was also evident from the pulsation. It was insinuated to me that man is kept engaged by the angels in the pious and holy thoughts which he entertained at the point of death; and it was also insinuated that those who are dying usually think about eternal life, and seldom of salvation and happiness, and therefore the angels keep them in the thought of eternal life. In this thought they are kept for a considerable time by the celestial angels before these angels depart, and those who are being resuscitated are then left to the spiritual angels, with whom they are next associated. Meanwhile they have a dim idea that they are living in the body. As soon as the internal parts of the body grow cold, the vital substances are separated from the man . . . nothing vital can be left behind.[81]

One wonders whether Swedenborg was saying that the vital organs and fluids would be needed in the afterlife. If so, this sounds more like an ancient Egyptian burial rite, complete with mummification, than a Christian vision of life after death:

The celestial angels who sat at the head remained with me for some time after I was, as it were, resuscitated, but they conversed only tacitly. It was perceived from their cogitative speech that they made light of all fallacies and falsities, smiling at them not indeed as matters for derision, but as if they cared nothing about them. Their speech is cogitative, devoid of sound, and in this kind of language they begin to speak with the souls with whom they are at first present. As yet the man, thus resuscitated by the celestial angels, possesses only an obscure life; but when the time comes for him to be delivered to the spiritual angels, then after a little delay, when the spiritual angels have approached, the celestial [ones] depart; and it has been shown me how the spiritual angels operate in order that the man may receive the benefit of light.[82]

Swedenborg described how the celestial angels work on the dead human and bring him or her toward a new life:

I was shown how these angels work. They seemed as it were to roll off the coat of the left eye toward the septum of the nose, in order that the eye might be opened and the use of light granted. To the man it appears as if this were really done, but it is only an appearance. After this little membrane has been in appearance rolled off, some light is visible, but dim such as a man sees through his eyelids when he first awakes out of sleep; and he who is being resuscitated is in a tranquil state, being still guarded by the celestial angels. There then appears a kind of shadow of an azure color, with a little star, but I perceived that this takes place with variety. Afterwards there seems to be something gently unrolled from the face, and perception is communicated to him, the angels being especially cautious to prevent any idea coming from him but such as is of a soft and tender nature, as of love; and it is now granted him to know that he is a spirit. He then commences his life. This at first is happy and glad, for he seems to himself to have come into eternal life, which is represented by a bright white light that becomes of a beautiful golden tinge, by which is signified his first life, to wit, that it is celestial as well as spiritual. His being next taken into the society of good spirits is represented by a young man sitting on a horse and directing it towards hell, but the horse cannot move a step. He is represented as a youth because when he first enters upon eternal life he is among angels, and therefore appears to himself to be in the flower of youth.[83]

This description may be one of the very first of its kind. It certainly comes close to what have since been described as many thousands of "near-death" experiences, which today are chronicled in books and shown on certain television programs (to learn more about these experiences, simply enter the keywords "near death experiences" and "afterlife" into any Internet search engine and browse the many sites listed). As a scientist, Swedenborg described the experience much more carefully and in greater depth than the average person. Thus, his announcing of the "bright white light that becomes of a beautiful golden tinge" comes late in the story rather than at the beginning.

Swedenborg also described hell in all its varieties. His basic premise was that no one is thrown into hell by God's command. Rather, the individual is drawn to heaven or hell based on what he or she was like in worldly life. If the person was naturally friendly and helpful, then he or she will want to ascend to heaven where all the angels work together for the good of the whole. If the person was grasping, resentful, or deceitful, then he or she would naturally *choose* to go to the lower regions.

NEAR-DEATH EXPERIENCES

Dr. Raymond Moody published *Life After Life* in 1975. Since then, thousands, perhaps hundreds of thousands, of Americans have testified to having experienced a partial passage toward death.

Most of those who write or speak about these experiences make the process seem shorter and perhaps easier than what Swedenborg described in *Heaven and Its Wonders and Hell*. Swedenborg, who was still at least partly a scientist, gave greater and longer descriptions than those that are usually given today. His findings concurred with many modern accounts in that there was a new, bright white light and that sometime in the process, the person experiences a "life review."

American interest in the afterlife has grown by leaps and bounds since Raymond Moody published his book. Around the year 2000, millions of Americans became familiar with a television program called *Crossing Over With John Edwards*. Edwards, a self-described psychic medium, appeared to connect with the deceased loved ones of members of the audience. Sometimes his connections appeared faulty or incomplete, but there were also many times when audience members gasped after he told them that a departed uncle or aunt wanted them to "mind the groceries" or to "get rid of that old car and get a new one." Through such seemingly trivial connections, many people came to believe that they had made contact with their relatives or friends on the other side.

Swedenborg painted a frightening picture of what sometimes happened to couples who were married on Earth but whose natures were at war with one another:

> The collision and antagonism of the interiors of such are disclosed after their death, when commonly they come together and fight like enemies and tear each other; for they then act in accordance with the state of the interiors. Frequently I have been permitted to see them fighting and tearing each other, sometimes with great vengeance and cruelty. For in the other life everyone's interiors are set at liberty; and they are no longer restrained by outward bounds and worldly considerations, everyone then being just what he is interiorly."[84]

This expression "everyone's interiors are set at liberty" appears time and again in Swedenborg's descriptions of heaven and hell. Swedenborg insisted on this point—that one's nature, for good or ill, became expanded in its power in the afterlife. Such liberty in the afterlife presupposes that a man or woman should do his or her best to learn restraint in *this* lifetime.

Swedenborg made a similar point when it came to his remarks on "After Death":

> It has been proved to me by manifold experience that when man passes from the natural world into the spiritual, as he does when he dies, he carries with him all his possessions, that is, everything that belongs to him as a man, except his earthly body. For when man enters the spiritual world or the life after death, he is in a body as he was in the world, with no apparent difference, since he neither sees nor feels any difference. But his body is then spiritual, and thus separated or purified from all that is earthly; and when what is spiritual touches or sees what is spiritual, it is just the same as when what is natural touches or sees what is natural. So when a man has become a spirit he does not know that he has died, but believes that he is in the same body that he had in the world.[85]

Finally, Swedenborg described his vision of hell:

> An opinion has prevailed with some that God turns away His
> face from man, casts man away from Himself, and casts him into
> hell, and is angry on account of his evil; and some believe also
> that God punishes man and does evil to him. In this opinion
> they establish themselves by the sense of the letter of the Word,
> where such things are declared, not knowing that the spiritual
> sense of the Word, by which the sense of the letter is made clear,
> is wholly different; and consequently that the genuine doctrine
> of the church, which is from the spiritual sense of the Word,
> teaches otherwise, namely that God never turns away His face
> from man, and never casts man away from Himself, that He
> casts no one into hell and is angry with no one. [86]

This was much more comforting than the average theological
work. Most men and women of the eighteenth century believed
in hell and believed that God cast people into the infernal
depths. Swedenborg, in contrast, asserted that men and women
arrived in hell only through their own addiction to depravity
and that God was always eager to redeem each and every soul.

Evildoing in the world leads to a continuation of such behav-
ior, Swedenborg taught. If we carry all our faculties and behaviors
with us into the afterlife, it makes sense that we would bring our
attractions, lusts, and addictions. Even then, there is still hope, for
a person can turn away from his or her previous ties. According
to Swedenborg, however, many people remain attracted to what
attracted them in worldly life and slowly bring themselves to hell.
Swedenborg's descriptions of existence there are chilling:

> Those who in the life of the body have contracted a habit of
> saying one thing and thinking another, especially those who
> under the appearance of friendship have longed for the
> possessions of others, wander about, and wherever they come
> ask whether they may stay there, saying that they are poor;
> and when they are received from innate desire long for all

they see. As soon as their character is detected they are driven out and fined; and sometimes they are miserably wracked in various ways in accordance with the deceitful simulation which they have contracted, some being wracked in the whole body, some in the feet, some in the loins, some in the breast, some in the head, and some only in the region of the mouth.[87]

Swedenborg then hastened to point out one's responsibility in being in hell:

It is to be observed that in the other life no one undergoes any punishment and torture on account of his hereditary evil, but only on account of the actual evils which he himself has committed. When the evil are being punished, angels are always present who moderate the punishment and alleviate the pains of the sufferers, but cannot take them away. For there is such an equilibrium in the other life that evil punishes itself, and unless it could be taken away by means of punishment, those in whom it exists could not but be kept in some hell to eternity.[88]

So far as we know, Swedenborg never read any Hindu or Buddhist texts, but his writing on hell, and especially his belief in the "equilibrium in the other life," suggests that he knew something of the ideas of karma and reincarnation. The idea that the soul migrates from one lifetime to another, and that it picks up merits and demerits along the way, is familiar to Western readers today, but this was not the case in Swedenborg's time.

In *Heaven and Its Wonders and Hell,* Swedenborg depicted a ceaselessly intricate pattern of movement in the other worlds. Swedenborg the scientist had been absolutely convinced that nothing was separate in nature; anything separate would quickly wither and die. He brought this scientific idea to his study of the afterlife; the result was that he perceived heaven and hell as full of intimate connections, all of which stemmed from a person's life on Earth.

8

The Last
Years

*Such angels, as soon as they hear
Divine truths, will and do them.*

—Emanuel Swedenborg,
Heaven and Its Wonders and Hell

S wedenborg was now more taken up than ever with spiritual things. But he remained very much a Swede, conscious of his country's position on the northern fringe of Europe and comfortable in its neutrality. The great Seven Years' War broke out in 1756, pitting most of the European powers against each other. Sweden stayed out of the war, though many of its sons sold their services as mercenaries to one side or the other. In the midst of this great war, Swedenborg was taken up with inner matters. But this changed, however briefly, in the summer of 1759. Swedenborg's most celebrated act of clairvoyance, or clear sightedness, was about to occur.

The following excerpt from Benjamin Worcester's *The Life and Mission of Emanuel Swedenborg* recounts an experience Swedenborg had while visiting a friend 300 miles away from his home in Stockholm. Despite the great distance between his friend's house in Gottenburg and his home in Stockholm, Swedenborg received some kind of psychic knowledge of a fire occurring in his hometown:

> In the year 1759, towards the end of July, on Saturday at four o'clock P.M., Swedenborg arrived at Gottenburg from England, when Mr. William Castel invited him to his house, together with a party of fifteen persons. About six o'clock Swedenborg went out, and returned to the company quite pale and alarmed. He said that a dangerous fire had just broken out in Stockholm, in the Sodermalm (Gottenberg is about three hundred miles from Stockholm), and that it was spreading very fast. He was restless and went out often. He said that the house of one of his friends, whom he named, was already in ashes, and that his own was in danger. At eight o'clock, after he had been out again, he joyfully exclaimed, "Thank God! the fire is extinguished, the third door from my house." The news occasioned great commotion through the whole city, but particularly amongst the company in which he was. It was announced to the governor the same evening. On Sunday morning Swedenborg was summoned to the governor,

who questioned him concerning the disaster. Swedenborg described the fire precisely—how it had begun, and in what manner it had ceased, and how it had continued. On the same day the news spread through the city, and, as the governor had thought it worthy of attention, the consternation was considerably increased, because many were in trouble on account of their friends and property which might have been involved in the disaster. On Monday evening a messenger arrived at Gottenburg, who was dispatched by the Board of Trade during the time of the fire. In the letters brought by him the fire was described precisely in the manner stated by Swedenborg.[89]

One can, of course, be skeptical. Reports like this are sometimes created in the aftermath of a major event, giving a person an undeserved prophet-like status. This report, however, was written for the German philosopher Immanuel Kant, and there is every likelihood that it was true.

By about 1760, Swedenborg had settled into a comfortable routine at home. Having spent many years abroad and many years in the realm of spirits and visions, he now tried to relax by gardening.

One year later, in 1761, Swedenborg went to a court function. Queen Louisa Ulrika inquired whether Swedenborg had seen her late brother, a former prince of Prussia, in the afterlife. In his grave, somber manner, Swedenborg replied that he had not done so, but that he would look for him.

Two or three weeks later, Swedenborg went to the royal apartments for another court function. This time, he did not wait to be announced but went straight to the queen's quarters. In private, he told her he had met her deceased brother and that the brother had a message for her. Soon after they spoke, the queen was seen to have an altered complexion. She told some of her servants, "This no mortal could have told me!"[90]

Years passed. Swedenborg was now in his late seventies. He probably hoped to live a few more years and then pass over to the other side in peace. Events turned in a different direction.

**EMANUEL
SWEDENBORG**

Emanuel Swedenborg became a student at the University of Uppsala in 1704. Uppsala, which was one of Sweden's only two universities at the time, was the setting for Swedenborg's initial contact with the works of major intellectuals such as Isaac Newton and René Descartes.

King Charles XII ruled the throne during Swedenborg's early adulthood. Charles was known as a warrior king and spent a significant portion of his time as monarch either in battle or exile. When both Swedenborg and the king returned from their individual journeys abroad, Charles would become a patron of Swedenborg's work.

John Flamsteed was one of the leaders of the English Royal Society. A major British scientist, Flamsteed was considered the best astronomer in the country and Swedenborg became acquainted with him while living in London. The pair soon developed a working relationship and tackled many astronomical problems together.

It was in the Royal Observatory at Greenwich that Swedenborg spent many nights gazing at the sky, cataloging stars and recording celestial movements. Swedenborg later focused his attention on determining longitude using astronomy.

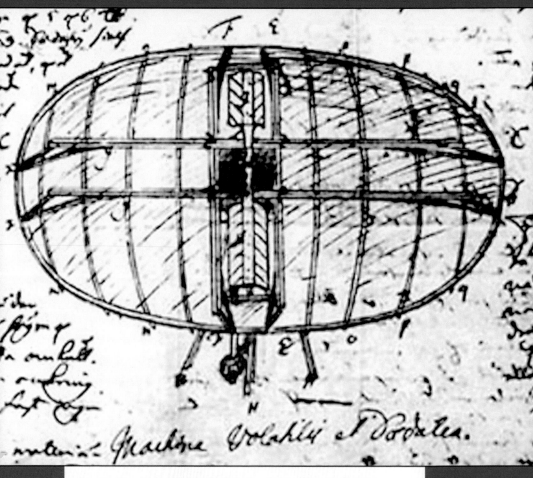

Swedenborg drafted this sketch of his "Daedalian" or "Machine for Flying" in 1714. Considering the technology available during Swedenborg's life, the design is remarkably modern in its aeronautical shape and inclusion of landing gear and even a device for control. A replica of one of Swedenborg's designs can be found in the Early Flight section of the Smithsonian Museum in Washington, D.C., today.

Swedenborg and his mentor Christopher Polhem drew up the plans for the Trollhattan Locks in the early eighteenth century, but the work was not completed until 1918. The locks, which adjust the water level to allow ships to pass through, made it possible for Swedish ships to travel between the Baltic and North Seas without passing Danish ports.

Toward the end of the 1760s, Swedenborg, for the first time, came into conflict with the Swedish Lutheran Church.

CHARGES OF HERESY

For many years, Swedenborg had attended few church services. He had also made some intemperate comments about some of the Swedish clergy. Once, when someone asked him about the state of a recently deceased clergyman, Swedenborg replied that he had gone straight to hell. The man, it seemed, had acted in a godly and generous fashion only when he was in the pulpit; the rest of the time, he celebrated his vanity, pride, and avarice. Remarks such as this one naturally offended many members of the Swedish clergy.

That Swedenborg was not accosted by the Lutheran Church until late in life may be attributable to his family connections. His father had been a bishop, and through his brother-in-law Eric Benzelius, Swedenborg was related to many of the leading members of the Swedish Church. In 1769, however, a number of church leaders began to accuse some of his followers of heresy (interestingly, the charge was never actually brought against Swedenborg himself).

The Swedish Lutheran Consistory examined the case. Although there were numerous persons who testified to Swedenborg's good character, the consistory found that many of his writings were in error, especially the ones that referred to conversations with angels. The consistory forwarded this finding to the king. King Adolphus Frederic sent a royal resolution to the consistory on January 2, 1770:

> Our chancellor of justice in a humble memorial has reported to us the stir which the theological writings of Emanuel Swedenborg, and the so-called Swedenborgianism which thence has taken its rise, have caused in the diocese which has been graciously entrusted to your charge. . . . In respect to the importance and delicate nature of this matter, it is likewise our desire to enjoin you to have a watchful eye upon all theological works announced

for publication . . . further, that reviews or translations of Swedenborg's works, or of other similar writings, which contain anything conflicting with our pure doctrine, are not to be passed without your most careful examination; especially when not written in the Latin language.[91]

Swedenborg protested his innocence and asked to be allowed to demonstrate his loyalty to the Church and to the Crown. This opportunity was not provided, and in the summer of 1771, Swedenborg left his native land for the last time. He traveled to England where he intended to publish another of his theological works. Swedenborg very likely left Sweden with some sadness in his heart. It was his homeland, the one he had served for many years, and it was where his theology had been condemned without his having a proper chance to defend himself.

One of the last Swedes to see Swedenborg before he left home was General Christian Tuxen. The general was on a ship off Sweden's western coast when he learned that Swedenborg was on board. Remembering their earlier conversations, Tuxen went at once to Swedenborg's cabin where he found:

The Assessor seated in undress, his elbows on the table, his hands supporting his face, which was turned towards the door, his eyes open and much elevated. I was so imprudent as immediately to address him, expressing my happiness at seeing and speaking with him. At this he recovered himself, for he had really been in a trance . . . from which, however, he soon recovered, bidding me welcome and asking me whence I came. I answered that as I had heard he was on board a Swedish ship lying below the Koll, I had come to invite him on the part of my wife and myself to favor us with his company at our house. To this he immediately consented, pulling off his gown and slippers, putting on clean linen, and dressing himself as briskly and alertly as a young man of one and twenty. He told the captain where he was to be found if the wind became favorable, and accompanied me to Elsinore. Here my wife, who was

then indisposed, was waiting to welcome him and to request
him to excuse us if our house should in any respect fall short
of our wishes to entertain him, adding that she had for these
thirty years been afflicted with a violent hysterical disease,
which occasioned her much pain and uneasiness. He very
politely kissed her hand and answered "Oh dear! Of this we
will not speak; only acquiesce in the will of God; it will pass
away and you will again attain the same health and beauty as
when you were fifteen years of age." [92]

Swedenborg did not tell the lady that she would soon pass away.

A PROPHET LEAVES HIS HOMELAND FOR GOOD

Settling in London, Swedenborg involved himself in the publication of his *Apocalypse Revealed*. In the early winter of 1771–1772,
he suffered a stroke that caused a paralysis of his left side. He
recovered in about 10 days and went back to work. During
this time, he lived at the house of Richard Shearsmith on
Great Bath Street.

Mr. Shearsmith's maid later recalled that Swedenborg had
predicted the date and time of his death. He had calmly
informed her and several of his friends that he would die at
5:00 P.M. on March 29, 1772. She remembered that as he spoke
of this, Swedenborg was as pleased as if he were planning to go
on vacation. On the day mentioned, he heard the afternoon
bell chime and asked her what time it was. When she replied
that it was five o'clock, he replied, "dat be good, me tank you;
God bless you." About 10 minutes later, he was dead. [93]

Swedenborg's life stopped, but the world went on. He had
lived for so long at the intersection of the two worlds that he felt
as comfortable leaving the physical one as he would have felt
slipping into a new pair of shoes.

9

Swedenborg's Legacy

This no mortal could have told me!

—Swedish Queen Louisa Ulrika,
on her conversation with Swedenborg

N either London nor Stockholm made very much of Sweden-borg's death. His obituary in the London *Times* was brief in the extreme, and Sweden's government seemed glad to be rid of this philosopher who had stirred up trouble toward the end of his life.

Only a few friends and associates took the time to compose memorials about the man they missed. One was Count A. J. von Hopken, a member of the Swedish Senate and for a time the prime minister of the nation. He wrote to General Tuxen:

> I have not only known [Swedendorg] these two and forty years, but, also, some time since, daily frequented his company. A man like me has lived long in the world and even in an extensive career of life, must have had numerous opportunities of knowing men as to their virtues or vices, their weakness or strength; and in consequence thereof I do not recollect to have known any man of more uniformly virtuous character than Swedenborg—always contented, never fretful or morose, although throughout his life his soul was occupied with sublime thoughts and speculations. . . . He was without contradiction the most learned man in my country.[94]

Another memorial came from the Reverend Arvid Ferelius in London. Writing to his friend, a professor at Griefswalde in Sweden, Ferelius explained:

> Assessor Swedenborg died in the month of March, 1772, and was buried by me on April 5th in the burying vault of the Swedish Ulrica-Eleonora church. . . . I visited him several times, and asked him each time whether he had an idea that he was to die at this time, upon which he answered, "Yes." Upon this I observed to him, that as quite a number of people thought that his sole purpose in promulgating his new theological system had been to make himself a name, or to acquire celebrity, which object indeed he had thereby

attained—if such had been the case, he ought now to do the world the justice to retract it either in whole or in part, especially as he could not expect to derive any additional advantage from this world, which he would soon leave. He thereupon half rose in his bed, and laying his sound hand upon his breast said, with some manifestation of zeal, "As true as you see me here before your eyes, so true is everything that I have written; and I could have said more, had it been permitted. When you enter eternity, you will see everything, and then you and I shall have much to talk about."[95]

This assertion had been quite necessary since many leaders of new religious sects sometimes apologize for their conduct, admitting that they had done things and written things in order to gain attention. Clearly, Swedenborg faced death with no similar intention.

One of the great questions of Swedenborg's life was coined by the American psychologist Wilson Van Dusen. Van Dusen discovered Swedenborg's work in the 1960s. A few years later, Van Dusen was a clinical psychologist at Mendocino State Hospital in California. He found a marked similarity between the delusional states of his patients and the states that Swedenborg reported in many of his books. Van Dusen could render a full appreciation of Swedenborg because the findings of Sigmund Freud and Carl Jung had been well published and spread during Van Dusen's lifetime.

Van Dusen was struck by the fact that there were orders and levels to the delusions and hallucinations of his patients; there were lower orders and higher orders of tormenters in the spiritual world. He looked back at Swedenborg's writings and found a remarkable congruity between Swedenborg's reports and those of his own patients. To be absolutely clear about his findings, Van Dusen posed a question to which he provided some interesting answers:

> Could Swedenborg have been mad? There is simply no evidence for this. In contrast to the limited, impaired,

unproductive lives of these patients, his life was one of the richest and most productive ever lived. He explored voluntarily what patients are involuntarily thrown into. . . . My guess is that the spiritual world is much as Swedenborg described it, and is the unconscious. We are mostly unconscious of the other spiritual worlds. It is meant to be that way, for it is very dangerous when these worlds are opened up to man, just as Swedenborg said. He did not advocate that anyone try to follow him. My guess is that Swedenborg systematically explored the same worlds that psychotic patients find themselves thrust into, and these worlds are heaven and hell, the worlds beyond this one, inside this one. It is not too surprising, when you think of it, that persons who are disordered inwardly experience some of the raw underpinning of experience that are invisible to the smoothly functioning mind.[96]

Swedenborg's thoughts and words lived on long after his death. His ideas were largely rejected in Sweden, but this was not the case in London and Amsterdam, the two cities Swedenborg had visited the most. London, especially, was home to a small group of true believers in Swedenborg's philosophy; about 15 years after his death, they formed the first New Jerusalem Church.

One of the people who signed the agreement to start the church was a painter and poet named William Blake. Born in London in 1757, the very year that Swedenborg had claimed would see the Last Judgment, Blake grew up in poverty and pain. His earnest and artistic soul demanded an answer to the pain of life, but not a material one. He wanted a spiritual answer, and he found the first one in the new church of Swedenborg's followers (it is important not to call it Swedenborg's church since he sought no followers during his lifetime).

Blake blossomed as a painter and poet during the 1790s. He also rejected much of Swedenborg's philosophy during this decade. Where once he had seen a doctrine that promised freedom and liberation, he now saw a doctrine too established within its beliefs. As a result, Blake published his *Heaven and Hell* in 1793.

Artists and art historians have ever since seen *Heaven and Hell* as one of Blake's most significant works. He developed a case against Swedenborg, demonstrating that Swedenborg had created a doctrine too firm in its beliefs to allow for freedom. Blake, however, did not totally renounce the man behind the philosophy. In one of the most sensational of the artworks in his book, Blake hinted at his indebtedness to Swedenborg. In large handwriting at the bottom of the page are the words, "In Opposition Lies True Friendship."[97]

As much as the work contradicted Swedenborg on the face of things, we imagine that the Swedish philosopher would have heartily approved of these words. During his life, Swedenborg had had to break away from many people and doctrines, including those of his father and those of his fellow scientists. "In Opposition Lies True Friendship" could almost be a code expression for Swedenborgian beliefs.

As might be expected, Swedenborg's followers attracted only a small number of adherents. Significantly, many of them appeared on the American side of the Atlantic. The New World was generally more receptive to new doctrines, and Swedenborg's teachings found a small but eager audience in New England soon after the turn of the nineteenth century.

A small handful of Harvard students provided the impulse. Sampson Reed, a member of the Harvard class of 1818, was the leader. He delivered a master's speech on Swedenborg in 1821 and deeply impressed a few young Harvard men, one of whom, Samuel Worcester, would spend much of the rest of his life in unofficial Swedenborgian studies. His biography of Swedenborg remains one of the best even today. Another Harvard student in attendance was Ralph Waldo Emerson.

Deeply moved by Sampson Reed's commencement speech, Emerson went on to read Swedenborg at length. He compiled his deepest feelings on the subject in the book *Representative Men*, published in Boston in 1850. Emerson chose Swedenborg as one

of a handful of men who impacted their own times and who continued to have an effect long after their deaths. In *Representative
Men*, Emerson gave one of the most lasting tributes ever written
in Swedenborg's honor:

> A colossal soul, he lies vast abroad on his times, uncompre-
> hended by them, and requires a long focal distance to be seen;
> suggests, as Aristotle, Bacon, Selden, Humboldt, that a certain
> vastness of learning, or quasi omnipresence of the human soul
> in nature, is possible. His superb speculation, as from a tower,
> over nature and arts, without ever losing sight of the texture
> and sequence of things, almost realizes his own picture, in the
> *Principia*, of the original integrity of man.[98]

Emerson was clearly more comfortable with Swedenborg the
Man of Science than with Swedenborg the Mystic. All the same,
he allowed for the greatness that was encompassed in both sides
of the same person.

JOHNNY APPLESEED

Emanuel Swedenborg died in March 1772. Just two years later, John
Chapman was born in Leominster, Massachusetts. While there is no
direct connection between these two men, Chapman was deeply
influenced by Swedenborg.

Drawn to the frontier, Chapman moved west at an early age. He
was in the Ohio region by about 1800, and stories began to develop
about the oddly dressed frontiersman who sold bags of apple seeds
to newcomers. He wanted people to plant these seeds, grow great
apple trees, and make Ohio a wonderful place in which to live.

This part of the story is well known. What is less known is that
during his travels tending his orchards, John Chapman also handed out
pages of Swedenborgian literature. *Heaven and Its Wonders and Hell* was
available then, and parts of the *Arcana Caelestial* may have been, too.
John Chapman handed out this literature and dispensed pieces of
Swedenborgian wisdom to the people he met. Like Swedenborg
himself, Chapman advised kindness, humility, and a charitable spirit.

Emerson himself was one of the leaders of the Transcendental Movement in the United States. That movement did not officially adopt Swedenborg as one of its mentors, but Swedenborgian influence can be seen in the essays of Henry David Thoreau, in the sermons of some of the Unitarian ministers of the time, and even in the funerary art of the nineteenth century. After 1860, the Transcendental Movement faded, and less and less was heard of Swedenborg. Only a handful of Romantic poets, men like Vachel Lindsay, said much about Swedenborg.

Nevertheless, educated people continued to discover Swedenborg and his writings. One of these individuals, the French critic and poet Paul Valery, posed one of the most articulate of all questions concerning Swedenborg in 1936:

> How is a Swedenborg possible? What must be assumed to consider the coexistence of the qualities of a learned engineer, of an eminent government official, of a man who was wise in practical matters and learned in every field, with the character-istics of a visionary who has no hesitation in writing out and publishing visions, in allowing himself to be known as one visited by the inhabitants of another world, taught by them, and living a part of his life in their mysterious company? [99]

Swedenborg was first, and foremost, a man of hard, cool, rational science. The new scientific movement of the eighteenth century was developing when he studied at the University of Uppsala, and he was deeply affected by the move toward a scientific explanation of Man and the Universe.

Second, Swedenborg was a man of exploration. As assessor for the Swedish Bureau of Mines, he spent much time in mines, delving into crevices and experimenting with new ways of finding ore. This emphasis on exploration and experimen-tation led him, without his having planned it, into the realm of dreams and mysticism.

The great turning point, as shown in chapter one, was the series of dreams that he experienced in the spring of 1744.

Another type of scientist, more insistent on his rational mind, might have rejected the dreams. But Swedenborg had long since decided to follow wherever his mind led him, and he jumped into the exploration of his subconscious with the same enthusiasm that he had plumbed the nooks and crannies of the Swedish mines.

Had Swedenborg not experienced his religious turnaround in 1744, he might have continued for another 28 years as a man of science. Since his mind was always geared toward the unusual or unlikely, he might have come to new and startling discoveries. Since he turned to religion and the path of mysticism, the question is pointless.

Could all his thoughts and feelings, developed over the last 28 years of his life have been a prolonged delusion? Of course. Might his thoughts and feelings, which were poured out to the world in *Heavenly Secrets* and *Heaven and Its Wonders and Hell*, have been absolutely legitimate? Certainly. Can we make a formal conclusion about Swedenborg's visions and dreams? No.

A final assessment of Swedenborg will have to wait for some time. In 1758, when *Heaven and Its Wonders and Hell* was published, few people believed in a near-death experience. Today, many do. Future discoveries may serve to illuminate Swedenborg's extensive travels of the mind, heart, and spirit.

APPENDIX

PREFACE TO *HEAVEN AND HELL*

The Lord, speaking in the presence of His disciples of the consummation of the age, which is the final period of the church, says near the end of what He foretells about its successive states in respect to love and faith:

Immediately after the tribulation of those days, the sun shall be darkened, and the moon shall not give her light, and the stars shall fall from heaven, and the powers of the heavens shall be shaken. And then shall appear the sign of the Son of man in heaven; and then shall all the tribes of the earth mourn; and they shall see the Son of man coming in the clouds of heaven with power and great glory. And He shall send forth His angels with a trumpet and a great sound; and they shall gather together His elect from the four winds, from the end to end of the heavens.

Those who understood these words according to the sense of the letter have no other belief than that during that latest period, which is called the final judgment, all these things are to come to pass just as they are described in the literal sense—that is, that the sun and moon will be darkened and the stars will fall from the sky, that the sign of the Lord will appear in the sky, and He Himself will be seen in the clouds, attended by angels with trumpets; and furthermore, as is foretold elsewhere, that the whole visible universe will be destroyed, and afterwards a new heaven with a new earth will come into being. Such is the opinion of most men in the church at the present day.

But those who so believe are ignorant of the arcana that lie hid in every particular of the Word. For in every particular of the Word there is an internal sense which treats of things spiritual and heavenly, not of things natural and worldly, such as are treated of in the sense of the letter. And this is true not only of the meaning of groups of words, it is true of each particular word. For the Word is written solely by correspondences, to the end that there may be an internal sense in every least particular of it. What that sense is can be seen from all that has been said and shown about it in the *Arcana Caelestia*; also from quotations gathered from that work in the explanation of The White Horse spoken of in the Apocalypse.

It is according to that sense that what the Lord says in the passage quoted above respecting His coming in the clouds of heaven is to be understood. The "sun" there that is to be darkened signifies the Lord in respect to love; the "moon" the Lord in respect to faith; "stars" knowledge of good and truth, or of love and faith; "the sign of the Son of man in heaven" the manifestation of Divine truth; "the tribes of the earth" that shall mourn, all things relating to truth and good or to faith and love; "the coming of the Lord in the clouds of heaven with power and glory" His presence in the Word, and revelation; "clouds" signifying the sense of the letter of the Word; and "glory" the internal sense of the Word; "the angels with a trumpet and great voice" signify heaven as a source of Divine truth.

All this makes clear that these words of the Lord mean that at the end of the church, when there is no longer any love, and consequently no faith, the Lord will open the internal meaning of the Word and reveal arcana of heaven. The arcana revealed in the following pages relate to heaven and hell, and also to the life of man after death. The man of the church at this date knows scarcely anything about heaven and hell or about his life after death, although all these matters are set forth and described in the Word; and yet many of those born within the church refuse to believe in them, saying in their hearts, "Who has come from that world and told us?"

Lest, therefore, such a spirit of denial, which especially prevails with those who have much worldly wisdom, should also infect and corrupt the simple in heart and the simple in faith, it has been granted me to associate with angels and to talk with them as man with man, also to see what is in the heavens and what is in the hells, and this for thirteen years; so now from what I have seen and heard it has been granted me to describe these, in the hope that ignorance may thus be enlightened and unbelief dissipated. Such immediate revelation is granted at this day because this is what is meant by the Coming of the Lord.

APPENDIX

AN EXCERPT FROM SWEDENBORG'S DISCUSSION OF GENESIS IN *ARCANA CAELESTIA*

From the mere letter of the Word of the Old Testament no one would ever discern the fact that this part of the Word contains deep secrets of heaven, and that everything within it both in general and in particular bears reference to the Lord, to His heaven, to the church, to religious belief, and to all things connected therewith; for from the letter or sense of the letter all that any one can see is that, to speak generally, everything therein has reference merely to the external rites and ordinances of the Jewish Church. Yet the truth is that everywhere in that Word there are internal things which never appear at all in the external things except a very few which the Lord revealed and explained to the Apostles; such as that the sacrifices signify the Lord; that the land of Canaan and Jerusalem signify heaven, on which account they are called the Heavenly Canaan and Jerusalem, and that Paradise has a similar signification.

The Christian world, however, is as yet profoundly unaware of the fact that all things in the Word both in general and in particular, nay, the very smallest particulars down to the most minute iota, signify and enfold within them spiritual and heavenly things, and therefore the Old Testament is but little cared for. Yet that the Word is really of this character might be known from the single consideration that being the Lord's and from the Lord it must of necessity contain within it such things as belong to heaven, to the church, and to religious belief, and that unless it did so it could not be called the Lord's Word, nor could it be said to have any life in it. For whence comes its life except from those things that belong to life, that is to say, except from the fact that everything in it both in general and in particular bears reference to the Lord, who is the very Life itself; so that anything which does not inwardly regard Him is not alive; and it may be truly said that any expression in the Word that does not enfold Him within it, that is, which does not in its own way bear reference to Him, is not Divine.

Without such a Life, the Word as to the letter is dead. The case in this respect is the same as it is with man, who—as is known in the Christian world—is both internal and external. When separated from the internal man, the external man is the body, and is therefore dead; for it is the internal man that is alive and that causes the external man to be so, the internal man being the soul. So is it with the Word, which, in respect to the letter alone, is like the body without the soul.

While the mind cleaves to the literal sense alone, no one can possibly see that such things are contained within it. Thus in these first chapters of Genesis, nothing is discoverable from the sense of the letter other than that the creation of the world is treated of, and the garden of Eden which is called Paradise, and Adam as the first created man. Who supposes anything else? But it will be sufficiently established in the following pages that these matters contain arcana which have never yet been revealed; and in fact that the first chapter of Genesis in the internal sense treats in general of the new creation of man, or of his regeneration, and specifically of the Most Ancient Church; and this in such a manner that there is not the least expression which does not represent, signify, and enfold within it these things.

That this is really the case no one can possibly know except from the Lord. It may therefore be stated in advance that of the Lord's Divine mercy it has been granted me now for some years to be constantly and uninterruptedly in company with spirits and angels, hearing them speak and in turn speaking with them. In this way it has been given me to hear and see wonderful things in the other life which have never before come to the knowledge of any man, nor into his idea. I have been instructed in regard to the different kinds of spirits; the state of souls after death; hell, or the lamentable state of the unfaithful; heaven, or the blessed state of the faithful; and especially in regard to the doctrine of faith which is acknowledged in the universal heaven. . . .

APPENDIX

EXCERPT FROM *THE HEAVENLY CITY: A SPIRITUAL GUIDEBOOK* (FROM PART I: GOODNESS AND TRUTH)

Everything in the universe that is in harmony with the divine plan relates to goodness and truth. Goodness and truth come from the divine, which is the source of everything. This means there cannot be anything in heaven or on earth that does not relate to these two things. With this in mind, we can see that nothing is more important than knowing what is good and what is true, and how the two are attracted to each other and united. Religious people especially should understand these things, since just as everything in heaven relates to goodness and truth, so does everything in religion. What is good and true in heaven is also good and true in religion. So I will begin with goodness and truth.

To be in harmony with the divine plan, goodness and truth should be united as one thing, not separated into two. They come from the divine together, they are together in heaven, and they should be together in religion, too.

In heaven, the relationship between goodness and truth is called heavenly marriage. All the angels there have this kind of marriage inside them. That is why heaven is compared to a marriage in the Bible. The Lord is called the bridegroom and husband, and heaven and religion are called the bride and wife. Heaven and religion are called this because the people in them accept divine goodness according to true ideas.

All the understanding and wisdom of the angels comes from this marriage. None of it comes from goodness separated from truth or truth separated from goodness. It is the same for religious people.

Since the relationship between goodness and truth takes the form of a marriage, we can see that goodness loves truth, and truth loves goodness. They want to be together. If we are religious but do not have this kind of love and desire, we do not have a heavenly marriage inside ourselves. This means religion is not yet inside us, since the relationship between goodness and truth makes religion.

There are many different kinds of goodness. In general, there is spiritual goodness, material-level goodness, and both together in genuine ethical goodness. There are the same kinds of truth as there are of goodness, because truth goes with goodness. It is the form goodness takes.

It is the same with evil and falsity as with goodness and truth, except that they are opposites. Everything in the universe that is in harmony with the divine plan relates to goodness and truth, but everything that is opposed to the divine plan relates to evil and falsity. Goodness and truth love to be together, and evil and falsity love to be together. And all understanding and wisdom grow out of the relationship between goodness and truth, but all irrationality and foolishness grow out of the relationship between evil and falsity. The relationship between evil and falsity is called hellish marriage.

Evil and falsity are the opposite of goodness and truth. So we can see that we cannot combine truth with evil, or goodness with falsity that comes from evil. If we connect truth to evil, it is no longer true, but false, because it becomes distorted. If we connect goodness to falsity that comes from evil, it is no longer good, but evil, because it becomes corrupted. However, falsity that does not come from evil can be combined with goodness.

When we rationalize and live out our bad traits and the false ideas we get from them, we cannot see what is good and true, since evil thinks of itself as good, and falsity thinks of itself as true. But if we strengthen and live out our good qualities and the true ideas we get from them, we can see what is evil and false.

This is why: all our good qualities and the true ideas that go with them are heavenly in essence—or if they are not, they still come from a heavenly source. But all our bad traits and the false ideas that go with them are hellish in essence—or if they are not, they still come from a hellish source. And everything heavenly is brightly lit, but everything hellish is in the dark.

APPENDIX

SWEDENBORG ON THE CONCEPT OF THE LAST JUDGMENT

Those who have not known the spiritual sense of the Word, have understood that everything in the visible world will be destroyed in the day of the Last Judgment; for it is said, that heaven and earth are then to perish, and that God will create a New Heaven and a New Earth. In this opinion they have also confirmed themselves because it is said that all are then to rise from their graves, and that the good are then to be separated from the evil, with more to the same purport. But this is said in the sense of the letter of the Word. . . .

He who comprehends the Word only according to the sense of the letter, may be led into various opinions, as indeed has been the case in the Christian world, where so many heresies have thus arisen, and every one of them is confirmed from the Word. But since no one has hitherto known, that in the whole and in every part of the Word there is a spiritual sense, nor even what the spiritual sense is; therefore, they who have embraced this opinion concerning the Last Judgment are excusable.

But still they may now know, that neither the visible heaven nor the habitable earth will perish, but that both will endure; and that by "the New Heaven and the New Earth" is meant a New Church, both in the heavens and on the earth.

It is said a New Church in the heavens, for there is a church in the heavens, as well as on the earth; for there also is the Word, and likewise preaching, and Divine worship as on the earth; but with a difference—that there all things are in a more perfect state, because there they are not in the natural world, but in the spiritual; hence all there are spiritual men, and not natural as they were in the world. That it is so may be seen in the [my] work on Heaven and Hell. . . .

The passages in the Word, in which mention is made of the destruction of heaven and earth, are:

Lift up your eyes to heaven, and look upon the earth beneath; the heavens are about to perish like smoke, and the earth shall wax old like a garment (Isaiah 51:6).

Behold, I am about to create new heavens, and a new earth; neither shall the former things be remembered (Isaiah 65:17).

I will make new heavens and a new earth (Isaiah 66:22).

The stars of heaven have fallen to the earth, and heaven has departed like a book rolled together (Apocalypse 6:13, 14).

I saw a great throne, and One sitting thereon, from whose face the earth and the heaven fled away, and their place was not found (Apocalypse 20:11).

I saw a New Heaven and a New Earth, for the first heaven and the first earth had passed away (Apocalypse 21:1).

In these passages, by "a New Heaven" is not meant the visible heaven, but heaven itself where the human race is collected. . . . Every one who thinks from a somewhat enlightened reason may perceive that it is not the starry heaven, which is here meant, but that it is heaven in the spiritual sense, where angels and spirits are.

That by "the new earth" is meant a New Church on earth, has hitherto been unknown, for everyone by "earth" in the Word has understood the earth, when yet by it is meant the church; in the natural sense, earth is the earth, but in the spiritual sense it is the church, because they who are in the spiritual sense—that is, who are spiritual, as the angels are, when "the earth" is named in the Word—do not understand the earth itself, but the nation which is there, and its Divine worship; hence it is that by "earth" is signified the church. . . . I will here adduce one or two passages from the Word, by which in some measure it may be comprehended, that "earth" (land) signifies the church:

> The cataracts from on high were opened, and the foundations of the earth were shaken; in breaking, the earth is broken; in agitating, the earth is agitated; in reeling, the earth reels like a drunkard; it moves to and fro like a cottage; and heavy upon it is the transgression thereof (Isaiah 24:18–20).

> I will cause a man to be more rare than pure gold; therefore I will remove the heaven, and the earth shall be removed out of her place, in the day of the fierce anger of Jehovah (Isaiah 13:12, 13).

> The earth was agitated before Him, the heavens have trembled, the sun and the moon are become black, and the stars have withdrawn their splendor (Joel 2:10).

> The land was shaken and agitated, and the foundations of the mountains trembled and were shaken (Psalms 18:7, 8).

"To create" in the spiritual sense of the Word also signifies to form, to establish, and to regenerate; so by "creating a new heaven and a new earth" signifies to establish a New Church in heaven and on earth, as may appear from the following passages:

> The people who shall be created shall praise Jah (Psalms 102:18).

> Thou sendest forth the spirit, they are created; and Thou renewest the faces of the earth (Psalms 104:30).

> Thus said Jehovah, thy Creator, O Jacob, thy Former, O Israel, for I have redeemed thee, and I have called thee

by thy name, thou art Mine; everyone called by My name,
and for My glory I have created, I have formed him, yea,
I have made him (Isaiah 43:1, 7).

Hence it is that "the new creation" of man is his reformation,
since he is made anew, that is, from natural he is made spiritual;
and hence it is that "a new creature" is a reformed man.

1688   Emanuel Swedenborg born Emanuel Svedberg in Stockholm, Sweden.

1692   Reverend Jesper Svedberg takes a country parish.

1695   Reverend Svedberg becomes rector of the University of Uppsala.

1696   Sarah Behm Svedberg, Emanuel's biological mother, dies.

1697   Reverend Svedberg marries Sara Bergia; King Charles XI dies and is succeeded by his son, Charles XII.

1700   The Great Northern War begins; King Charles and his Swedish army defeat Russia in the Battle of Narva.

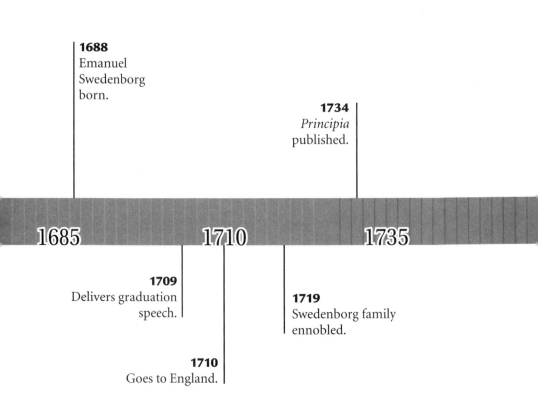

1688
Emanuel
Swedenborg
born.

1734
Principia
published.

1685   **1710**   **1735**

1709
Delivers graduation
speech.

1719
Swedenborg family
ennobled.

1710
Goes to England.

1703   Jesper Svedberg is made bishop of Skara; Emanuel Swedenborg stays in Uppsala with his sister Anna and her husband Eric Benzelius.

1709   Emanuel Swedenborg delivers his graduation speech at Uppsala; King Charles XII is decisively defeated by Russia in the Battle of Poltava.

1710   Swedenborg travels to England.

1711   Swedenborg meets some of the best minds in London.

1713   Swedenborg departs from London for Holland and then Paris.

1714   King Charles XII returns to Sweden from exile in Turkey.

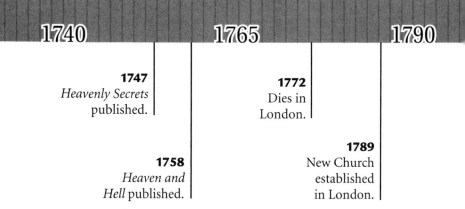

1741
On the Economy of the Animal Kingdom published.

1744
Has life-altering mystic experience.

1769
Heresy proceedings begin against Swedenborgian teachings.

1740

1765

1790

1747
Heavenly Secrets published.

1772
Dies in London.

1758
Heaven and Hell published.

1789
New Church established in London.

CHRONOLOGY

1715   Emanuel Swedenborg returns to Sweden.

1716   The first edition of *The Northern Inventor* (*Daedalus Hyperboreus*) is published.

1718   King Charles XII is killed in battle.

1719   "Era of Liberty" begins in Sweden; the Swedenborg family is ennobled and the children's last name is changed from Svedberg.

1720   Sara Bergia Svedberg dies, leaving much of her property to Emanuel.

1721   The Great Northern War ends with the Peace of Nystad.

1734   Swedenborg's *Principia* is published in Leipzig and Danzig.

1735   Bishop Jesper Svedberg dies.

1736   Swedenborg leaves Sweden for a four-year tour of Europe.

1741   Swedenborg's *On the Economy of the Animal Kingdom* is published; Sweden goes to war with Russia; Queen Ulrika Eleanora abdicates the throne in favor of her husband.

1743   A peace treaty is signed between Russia and Sweden; Swedenborg leaves home and travels to Holland.

1744   Swedenborg has a spiritual experience in Delft, Holland.

1747   Swedenborg retires from the Bureau of Mines.

1749   The first volume of *Heavenly Secrets* is published.

1756   The last volume of *Heavenly Secrets* is published.

1758   *Heaven and Hell* is published.

1758   William Blake is born in London.

1759   Swedenborg has a clairvoyant experience concerning a fire in Stockholm.

1764   Immanuel Kant publishes a devastating critique of *Heavenly Secrets*.

1769   Swedish Consistory starts heresy proceedings against Swedenborg's doctrine, but not against Swedenborg himself.

1770   Swedenborg leaves his homeland for the last time.

1771   Swedenborg suffers a stroke while in London.

1772   Swedenborg dies in London.

NOTES

CHAPTER 1:
Dreams and Visions

1. Benjamin Worcester, *The Life and Mission of Emanuel Swedenborg* (Boston: Roberts Brothers, 1892), p. 105.

2. Lars Berquist, *Swedenborg's Dream Diary*, trans. Anders Hallengren (New York: Swedenborg Foundation Publishers, 2001), p. 102.

3. Ibid., pp. 124-126.

4. Ibid., p. 126.

5. Ibid.

CHAPTER 2:
Young Swedenborg and Old Sweden

6. Robin Larsen, *Emanuel Swedenborg: A Continuing Vision* (New York: Swedenborg Foundation, 1988), p. 6.

7. William White, *Emanuel Swedenborg: His Life and Writings* (London: Simpkin, Marshall and Company, 1868), p. 6.

8. Benjamin Worcester, *The Life and Mission of Emanuel Swedenborg* (Boston: Roberts Brothers, 1892), p. 18.

9. Ibid.

10. Ibid., p. 19.

11. Ibid., pp. 22–23.

12. Larsen, p. 9.

13. R.M. Hatton, *Charles XII of Sweden* (New York: Weybright and Talley, 1968), p. 80.

14. Larsen, p. 11.

15. Sten Lindroth, *A History of Uppsala University, 1477–1977* (Uppsala, Sweden: Uppsala University, 1976), p. 65.

16. Signe Toksvig, *Emanuel Swedenborg: Scientist and Mystic* (New Haven, Conn.: Yale University Press, 1948), p. 38.

17. Ibid., p. 39.

18. Ibid., p. 40.

19. Ibid.

20. R.M. Hatton, *Charles XII of Sweden* (New York: Weybright and Talley, 1968), p. 294.

21. Ibid., pp. 305–310.

CHAPTER 3:
Adventures Abroad

22. Benjamin Worcester, *The Life and Mission of Emanuel Swedenborg* (Boston: Roberts Brothers, 1892, pp. 42–43.

23. R.L. Tafel, *Documents Concerning the Life and Character of Emanuel Swedenborg* (London: Swedenborg Society, 1890), vol. 1, pp. 206–208.

24. Worcester, pp. 35–36.

25. Dava Sobel and William J.H. Andrews, *The Illustrated Longitude* (New York: Walker and Company, 1995).

26. Worcester, pp. 35–36.

27. Ibid., pp. 42–43.

28. Ibid., p. 45.

CHAPTER 4:
The Mature Man of Science

29. Benjamin Worcester, *The Life and Mission of Emanuel Swedenborg* (Boston: Roberts Brothers, 1892), pp. 46-47.

30. Ibid.

31. William A. Johnson, trans., *Christopher Polhem, The Father of Swedish Technology* (Hartford, Conn.: Trinity College, 1963), pp. 3–7.

32. Ibid., pp. 13–17.

33. Ibid.

34. William White, *Emanuel Swedenborg: His Life and Writing* (London: Simpkin, Marshall and Company, 1868), p. 35.

35. Henry Soderberg, *Swedenborg's 1714 Airplane: A Machine to Fly in the Air* (New York: Swedenborg Foundation, 1988), p. 22.

36. White, p. 35.

37. Ibid., p. 36.

38. Signe Toksvig, p. 62.

39. R.M. Hatton, *Charles XII of Sweden* (New York: Weybright and Talley, 1968), p. 491.

40. A.F. Upton, *Charles XII and Swedish Absolutism* (Cambridge, U.K.: Cambridge University Press, 1998), p. 261.

CHAPTER 5:
The Great Change

41. Robin Larsen, *Emanuel Swedenborg: A Continuing Vision* (New York: Swedenborg Foundation, 1988), p 11.

42. William White, *Emanuel Swedenborg: His Life and Writings* (London: Simpkin, Marshall and Company, 1868), p. 43.

43. Benjamin Worcester, *The Life and Mission of Emanuel Swedenborg* (Boston: Roberts Brothers, 1892), p. 79.

44. Ibid., p, 84.

45. Ibid., p. 86.

46. James R. Rendell and Isiah Tansley, trans., Preface to *First Principles of Nature* (London: Swedenborg Society, 1912), p. xcv.

47. Ibid., pp. xcv–xcvi.

48. Ibid., p. xcvi.

49. Ibid., p. 42.

50. Ibid., p. 162.

51. Robin Larsen, *Emanuel Swedenborg: A Continuing Vision* (New York: Swedenborg Foundation, 1988), p. 35.

52. Emanuel Swedenborg, *The Economy of the Animal Kingdom, considered Anatomically, Physically, and Philosophically,* trans. Augustus Clissold (Boston: T.H. Carter and Sons, 1868), vol. 1, p. 1.

53. Ibid., p. 34.

54. Ibid., p. 92.

55. Ibid., pp. 85–86.

56. Ibid., vol. 2, p. 132.

57. Ibid., pp. 132–133.

58. Lars Berquist, *Swedenborg's Dream Diary*, trans. Anders Hallengren (New York: Swedenborg Foundation Publishers, 2001), pp. 133-134.

CHAPTER 6:
Heavenly Secrets

59. R.L. Tafel, *Documents Concerning the Life and Character of Emanuel Swedenborg* (London: Swedenborg Society, 1890), vol. 2, p. 493.

60. Emanuel Swedenborg, *Arcana Caelestia*, vol. 1, p. 1.

61. Ibid., p. 3.

62. Ibid., pp. 168–169.

63. Ibid., p. 214.

64. Ibid.

65. Ibid., vol. 2, p. 274.

66. Ibid., p. 386.

67. Ibid., p. 387.

68. Ibid., p. 464.

69. Ibid., pp. 465–466.

70. Immanuel Kant, *Dreams of a Spirit-Seer Illustrated by Dreams of Metaphysics*, trans. Emanuel F. Goerwitz and ed. Frank Sewall (New York: Macmillan Company, 1900), pp. 41–42.

71. Ibid., p. 46.

72. Ibid., p. 101.

CHAPTER 7:
Heaven and Hell

73. Emanuel Swedenborg, *Heaven and Its Wonders and Hell* (New York: The Citadel Press, 1965), p. 17.

74. Ibid.

75. Ibid., p. 19.

76. Ibid.

77. Ibid., p. 20.

78. Ibid., p. 22.

79. Ibid., p. 53.

80. Ibid., pp. 54–55.

81. Ibid., pp. 64–65.

82. Ibid., pp. 65–66.

83. Ibid., p. 66.

84. Ibid., p. 309.

85. Ibid., p. 391.

86. Ibid., p. 386.

87. Ibid., pp. 388–389.

88. Ibid.

NOTES

CHAPTER 8: The Last Years

89. Benjamin Worcester, *The Life and Mission of Emanuel Swedenborg* (Boston: Roberts Brothers, 1892).

90. Robin Larsen, *Emanuel Swedenborg: A Continuing Vision* (New York: Swedenborg Foundation, 1988), p 45.

91. R.L. Tafel, *Documents Concerning the Life and Character of Emanuel Swedenborg* (London: Swedenborg Society, 1890), pp. 318–319.

92. Worcester, pp. 330–331.

93. Ibid., p. 403.

CHAPTER 9:
Swedenborg's Legacy

94. Benjamin Worcester, *The Life and Mission of Emanuel Swedenborg* (Boston: Roberts Brothers, 1892), p. 332.

95. Ibid., p. 337.

96. Wilson Van Dusen, *The Presence of Other Worlds: The Psychological/Spiritual Findings of Emanuel Swedenborg* (New York: Harper & Row, 1974), pp. 135–137.

97. Robin Larsen, *Emanuel Swedenborg: A Continuing Vision* (New York Swedenborg Foundation, 1988), p. 93.

98. Ralph Waldo Emerson, *Representative Men* (Boston: Houghton Mifflin, 1892), p. 100.

99. Martin Lamm, *Emanuel Swedenborg: The Development of His Thought*, trans. Thomas Spiers and Anders Hallengren (New York: Swedenborg Foundation, 2002), p. xvii.

Assessor—An individual who determines the value of something; Swedenborg was one of the assessors of the Swedish Bureau of Mines

Cartesian—The system of thought derived from Rene Descartes

Celestial—Relating to Heaven

Corporeal—From the Latin word *corpus*, meaning "body"; therefore, to do with physical things

Correspondences—Refers to Swedenborg's belief that everything in the spiritual world has a corresponding figure in the natural world and vice versa

Deism—A theological approach popular in the eighteenth century; it viewed God as a great clockmaker who set the world in motion and then did not interfere with its events

Denary—Ten; In the case of mathematics, the system of numbers based on the number ten

Doctrine—A formal approach to religion, as in "Catholic doctrine," "Lutheran doctrine," and so forth

Dream Analysis—A tool of psychology used to understand the conscious mind by interpreting the workings of the subconscious; popularized by Sigmund Freud and Carl Jung in the early twentieth century

Heresy—Any religious belief that veers away from the doctrine of one's church

Holy Roman Empire—The empire created by the confederation of German and some Italian states from the tenth century until the eighteenth century

Lockean—The system of thought derived from the influential Enlightenment thinker John Locke; he believed in the goodness of humanity, progress through science, and the rights of the individual

GLOSSARY

Longitude—The east-west location of a person, place, or thing

Lutheran—A follower of Martin Luther, a Roman Catholic monk who published his famous *Ninety-Five Theses* protesting the abuses of the church in 1517, thereby igniting the Protestant Reformation; Swedenborg's father was a Lutheran bishop

Mystic—A person who has a direct personal experience of God

Near-Death Experience—A rare occurrence in which individuals who have died physically claim to experience the afterlife before being brought back to life; accounts of near-death experiences often include descriptions of a beautiful white light

Netherlands—Name for a kingdom of ten provinces in Western Europe, of which Holland is the best known

Newtonian—The system of thought derived from Isaac Newton, an English physicist, mathematician, and natural philosopher; Newton formulated laws of motion, gravitation, and optics, instilling in his followers a sense of order within the natural world

Ottoman—The Ottoman Turkish Empire, which ruled 1400 and 1910; during its lifetime it included territories in southeastern Europe, western Asia, and northern Asia

Prescience—Foresight; Swedenborg's most famous example was with the Stockholm fire of 1759

Swedenborgian—Refers to both a system of thought based on Swedenborg's theories as well as the church, set up within a generation after Swedenborg's death, formed by believers of that thought

Transcendentalists—Though the word encompasses thinkers from Plato's time, the term traditionally refers to a group of nineteenth-century American thinkers who believed in a realm of truth higher than that experienced by the senses or perceived by the senses; many of them, including intellectuals like Ralph Waldo Emerson and Henry David Thoreau, admired Swedenborg and his work

BOOKS

Benz, Ernst. *Emanuel Swedenborg: Visionary Savant in the Age of Reason*, trans. Nicholas Goodrick-Clarke. New York: Swedenborg Foundation, 2002.

Berquist, Lars. *Swedenborg's Dream Diary*, trans. Anders Hallengren. New York: Swedenborg Foundation Publishers, 2001.

Crompton, Anne Eliot. *Johnny's Trail*. New York: Swedenborg Foundation, 1983.

Emerson, Ralph Waldo. "Representative Men." In *Traits, Representative Men & Other Essays by Ralph Waldo Emerson*. New York: E. P. Dutton, 1908.

Hatton, R.M. *Charles XII of Sweden*. New York: Weybright and Talley, 1968.

Helander, Hans, ed. *Emanuel Swedenborg, Festivus Applauses in Caroli XII in Pomeraniam Suam Adventum*. Uppsala, Sweden: University of Uppsala, 1985.

Hobart, Nathaniel. *Life of Emanuel Swedenborg with Some Account of His Writings*. Boston: T.H. Carter and Company, 1844.

Johnson, William A., trans. and ed. *Christopher Polhem: The Father of Swedish Technology*. Hartford, Conn.: Trustees of Trinity College, 1963.

Kant, Immanuel. *Dreams of a Spirit-Seer Illustrated by Dreams of Metaphysics*, trans. Emanuel F. Goerwitz and ed. Frank Sewall. New York: Macmillan Company, 1900.

Lamm, Martin. *Emanuel Swedenborg: The Development of His Thought*, trans. Thomas Spiers and Anders Hallengren. New York: Swedenborg Foundation, 2002.

Larsen, Robin, ed. *Emanuel Swedenborg: A Continuing Vision*. New York: Swedenborg Foundation, 1988.

BIBLIOGRAPHY

Roberts, Michael. *The Age of Liberty: Sweden 1719–1772.* Cambridge, U.K.: Cambridge University Press, 1986.

Sobel, Dava, and William J. H. Andrews. *The Illustrated Longitude.* New York: Walker and Company, 1995.

Soderberg, Henry. *Swedenborg's 1714 Airplane: A Machine to Fly in the Air.* New York: Swedenborg Foundation, 1988.

Swedenborg, Emanuel. *Arcana Caelestia: Heavenly Aracana,* trans. J. Faulkner Potts and Rev. James R. Rendell. London: Swedenborg Society, 1967.

———. *The Economy of the Animal Kingdom,* trans. Augustus Clissold. Boston: T.H. Carter and Sons, 1868.

———. *Heaven and Its Wonders and Hell.* New York: The Citadel Press, 1965.

———. *Life After Death.* Bryn Athyn, Penn.: The New Church Press.

———. *Principia Rerum Naturalium,* trans. James R. Rendell and Isiah Tansley, 1953–1954.

———. *The True Christian Religion.* London: J.M. Dent & Sons, 1933.

Tafel, R.L. *Documents Concerning the Life and Character of Emanuel Swedenborg.* London: Swedenborg Society, 1890.

Toksvig, Signe. *Emanuel Swedenborg: Scientist and Mystic.* New Haven, Conn.: Yale University Press, 1948.

Trobridge, George. *Swedenborg: Life and Teaching.* New York: Swedenborg Foundation, 1951.

Upton, A.F. *Charles XI and Swedish Absolutism.* Cambridge, U.K.: Cambridge University Press, 1998.

Van Dusen, Wilson. *Emanuel Swedenborg's Journal of Dreams.* New York: Swedenborg Foundation, 1986.

———. *The Presence of Other Worlds: The Psychological/Spiritual Findings of Emanuel Swedenborg.* New York: Harper & Row, 1974.

White, William. *Swedenborg: His Life and Writings*. London: Simpkin, Marshall and Company, 1868.

Worcester, Benjamin. *The Life and Mission of Emanuel Swedenborg*. Boston: Roberts Brothers, 1892.

VIDEOS

Swedenborg: The Man Who Had to Know
Swedenborg Foundation, 1978

Splendors of the Spirit: Swedenborg's Quest for Insight
Swedenborg Foundation, 2001

INTERNET SOURCES

The Swedenborg Library. Available online at
http://www.newchurch.edu/college/facilities/library/greenbooks.html.

FURTHER READING

PRIMARY SOURCES

Kant, Immanuel. *Dreams of a Spirit-Seer Illustrated by Dreams of Metaphysics*, trans. Emanuel F. Goerwitz and ed. Frank Sewall. New York: Macmillan Company, 1900.

Swedenborg, Emanuel. *Arcana Caelestia: Heavenly Aracana*, trans. J. Faulkner Potts and Rev. James R. Rendell. London: Swedenborg Society, 1967.

———. *The Economy of the Animal Kingdom*, trans. Augustus Clissold. Boston: T.H. Carter and Sons, 1868.

———. *Heaven and Its Wonders and Hell.* New York: The Citadel Press, 1965.

———. *Life After Death.* Bryn Athyn, Penn.: The New Church Press.

———. *Principia Rerum Naturalium*, trans. James R. Rendell and Isaiah Tansley, 1953–1954.

———. *The True Christian Religion.* London: J.M. Dent & Sons, 1933.

SECONDARY SOURCES

Benz, Ernst. *Emanuel Swedenborg: Visionary Savant in the Age of Reason.* New York: Swedenborg Foundation, 2002.

Berquist, Lars. *Swedenborg's Dream Diary*, trans. Anders Hallengren. New York: Swedenborg Foundation Publishers, 2001.

Dole, George F. *A Scientist Explores Spirit: A Biography of Emanuel Swedenborg With Key Concepts of His Theology.* New York: Swedenborg Foundation, 1997.

Lamm, Martin. *Emanuel Swedenborg: The Development of His Thought*, trans. Thomas Spiers and Anders Hallengren. New York: Swedenborg Foundation, 2002.

Larsen, Robin, ed. *Emanuel Swedenborg: A Continuing Vision.* New York: Swedenborg Foundation, 1988.

Upton, A. F. *Charles XI and Swedish Absolutism*. Cambridge, U.K.: Cambridge University Press, 1998.

WEBSITES

The Swedenborg Association
http://www.swedenborg.net/

Organization that attempts to make Swedenborg's spiritual philosophies accessible to people from all different religious backgrounds.

The Swedenborg Foundation
http://www.swedenborg.com/

Publishes books relating to Swedenborg, his life, and his work.

The Swedenborg Movement
http://www.skipem.force9.co.uk/index.html

Group that works to spread the spiritual teachings of Swedenborg and to promote a better understanding of the spiritual leader and his work.

The Swedenborg Society
http://www.swedenborg.org.uk/contents.html

Organization dedicated to translating and printing the works of Emanuel Swedenborg throughout the world.

INDEX

INDEX

INDEX

SAMUEL WILLARD CROMPTON lives in the Berkshire Hills of western Massachusetts. His interest in Emanuel Swedenborg began when one of his sisters went to work for the Swedenborg Foundation in New York City. He is the author or editor of 30 books, including *Martin Luther, Thomas Merton,* and *Jonathan Edwards* in the SPIRITUAL LEADERS AND THINKERS series. He teaches American history and Western civilization at Holyoke Community College in Massachusetts.

MARTIN E. MARTY is an ordained minister in the Evangelical Lutheran Church and the Fairfax M. Cone Distinguished Service Professor Emeritus at the University of Chicago Divinity School, where he taught for thirty-five years. Marty has served as president of the American Academy of Religion, the American Society of Church History, and the American Catholic Historical Association, and was also a member of two U.S. presidential commissions. He is currently Senior Regent at St. Olaf College in Northfield, Minnesota. Marty has written more than fifty books, including the three-volume *Modern American Religion* (University of Chicago Press). His book *Righteous Empire* was a recipient of the National Book Award.